W9-AIA-284

"These materials are Bible-based and lead the new believer in an interactive, personal discovery process of God's purposes for fruitful and victorious living."

> Dr. John Orme, Executive Director,
> Interdenominational Foreign
> Mission Association

"Some of the best discipleship materials I have seen. I appreciate the centrality of Scripture and the Christ-centered focus."

> Dr. Hans Finzel, Executive Director,
> CBInternational

"The power of these books comes from the lifestyle of two people who practice these truths and teach them to others."

> Barry St. Clair, Founder and Director,
> Reach Out Ministries

"This discipleship curriculum is easy to read and easy to use. I heartily recommend it for [those] who desire to know Christ and make Him known."

> Dr. George Murray, President,
> Columbia International University,
> former General Director of
> The Evangelical Alliance Mission (TEAM)

DARING DISCIPLE SERIES

Knowing God

BILL JONES and TERRY POWELL

Christian Publications
CAMP HILL, PENNSYLVANIA

Christian Publications, Inc.
3825 Hartzdale Drive, Camp Hill, PA 17011
www.cpi-horizon.com
www.christianpublications.com

Faithful, biblical publishing since 1883

Knowing God
ISBN: 0-87509-880-0
LOC Catalog Control Number: 00-131980
© Copyright 2000 by
Crossover Communications International.

Printed in the United States of America

00   01   02   03   04   5   4   3   2   1

Unless otherwise indicated,
Scripture taken from the New American Standard Bible (NASB).
© The Lockman Foundation 1960, 1962, 1963,
1968, 1971, 1973, 1975, 1977, 1995.

For information, write:
Crossover Communications International
Box 211755
Columbia, SC USA 29221

Dedication

To Christen Ruth Jones
May you seek to love the Lord Jesus Christ
With all of your

- heart

- soul

- mind

- strength

Mark 12:30

And
To John Mark Powell
May you experience the ultimate purpose
of human existence: to glorify God
and to enjoy Him forever.

CONTENTS

Introduction

Knowing God is a Bible study guide for your individual benefit. This discipleship material will have maximum profit for you if you're a part of a group that meets on a weekly basis. A *Leader's Guide* for *Knowing God* is available from the publisher.

Other titles in the Daring Disciple Series include:

Discovering Your Identity
Walking in the Spirit
Learning to Trust
Sharing the Message

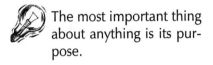 The most important thing about anything is its purpose.

Choosing a Life Purpose

Why do you get up in the morning? Imagine you posed that question to a wealthy Britisher born back in the 1800s. He would have answered that he had "devoted his life to trying to breed the perfect spotted mouse."[1]

You think this is a joke, don't you? But it's not. The man, who died just shy of his eighty-ninth birthday, didn't have to work for a living like the rest of us. So he was free to pursue any endeavor that interested him. For almost seventy adult years, he experimented with mice. Maybe he thought a spotted mouse would look prettier scurrying across the floor than a drab gray one. Maybe he figured a more colorful mouse would exhibit a friendly temperament and make a more affectionate pet. No one knows *why* he chose spotted mice as his life objective. But he did.

Q Briefly describe your reaction to the Britisher's story. What thoughts and feelings does it evoke?

A _____

_____

_____

_____

_____

Unless I miss my guess, his eccentric expenditure of time and energy shocks you, perhaps even repels you. You may be tempted to cry, "What a waste!" You think of more meaningful priorities or nobler causes, more altruistic investments of time and material resources.

A.W. Tozer, a prolific preacher and author during the first half of the twentieth century, read the man's story in an Associated Press article. Here's his reaction to the Britisher's preoccupation with the perfect spotted mouse:

> I cannot but grieve for my brother beyond the seas.
>
> Made in the image of God, equipped with awesome powers of mind and soul, called to dream immortal dreams and to think the long thoughts of eternity, he chooses the breeding of a spotted mouse as his reason for existing. Invited to walk with God on earth and to dwell at last with the saints and angels in the world above; called to serve his generation by the will of God, to press with holy vigor toward the mark for the prize of the high calling of God in Christ Jesus, he

dedicates his life to the spotted mouse—not just evenings or holidays, mind you, but his entire life.[2]

Up Close and Personal

Come to think of it, everybody lives according to some purpose. All human conduct is some philosophy of life gone off on an errand. If it isn't breeding spotted mice, it's stockpiling money. Pursuing a position of power or notoriety. Satisfying physical appetites. Something shoves everyone out of bed in the morning.

Q Allow me to get up close and personal. **What motivates *you*? What is your purpose in life?**

Before you answer, remember the means of identifying one's purpose: not by what a person says or writes, but how one lives. *An accurate purpose statement is constructed on the foundation of solid empirical evidence.*

Look in your rearview mirror at the past year. Analyze all your check stubs and cash transactions. Review every entry in your Day-Timer. Where did you direct your energies? What important decisions did you make? How did you treat the people in your sphere of influence? To what extent did you exercise your God-given abilities? What did you think about most constantly? On the basis of observable behavior, not some perceived ideal, summarize what appears to be your reason for existing.

_____

_____

_____

_____

_____

Was crafting a brief purpose statement more difficult than you expected? (To crystallize your thinking on such a substantive issue isn't a kindergarten-level exercise.) Or did you feel a twinge of conviction because your statement appears self-centered and temporal, rather than spiritual? If the exercise was either taxing or convicting, don't feel shot down. The fact that you are working on this chapter shows you are moving in the right direction as a Christian. The aim of the first two chapters of this discipleship book is to influence your thinking about a life purpose and to nudge you to revise it, as necessary.

Searching in the Wrong Places

How your "life purpose" reads depends on who or what shapes your values. What authority do you consult for guidance? What source provides the necessary grist for thinking about the direction of your life?

If Charles Colson is correct, a mushrooming number of people—including church members—are turning everywhere except to God in an effort to inject meaning into their existence.

> For a generation, Western society has been obsessed with the search for self. We have turned

the age-old philosophical question about the meaning and purpose of life into a modern growth industry. Like Heinz, there are fifty-seven varieties, and then some: biofeedback, yoga, creative consciousness . . . awareness workshops . . . each fad with an avid following until something new comes along.

Popular literature rides the wave with the best-selling titles that guarantee success with everything from making money to firming flabby thighs. This not-so-magnificent obsession to "find ourselves" has spawned a whole set of counterfeit values; to "live for success" as we "look out for number one," and we don't mind "winning through intimidation."

However, the "self" conscious world is in desperate straits. Each new promise leads only to a frustrating paradox. The 1970s self-fulfillment fads led to self-absorption and isolation, rather than the fuller, liberated lives they predicted. The technology created to lead humanity to this new promised land may instead obliterate us and our planet in a giant mushroom cloud. Three decades of seemingly limitless affluence have succeeded only in sucking our culture dry, leaving it spiritually empty and economically weakened. *Our world is filled with self-absorbed, frightened, hollow people . . .*

And in the midst of all this we have the church—those who follow Christ. For the church, this ought to be an hour of opportunity. The church alone can provide a moral vision to a wandering people; the church alone can step into the vacuum and demonstrate that there is a sovereign, living God who is the source of Truth.

BUT, the church is in almost as much trouble as the culture, for the church has bought into the same value system: Fame, success, materialism, and celebrity.[3]

Q Do you agree or disagree with Colson's assessment of the church? Why or why not?

A _____

_____

_____

_____

_____

There's just one compass accurate enough to help us navigate successfully through life. One logical place for us to go in order to understand our reason for existing. One reliable source that explains why men and women were plopped on planet earth to begin with. *The Bible.*

What is *God's* vision for the people He created? What is *God's* agenda for folks who claim kinship with Him? Formulating a clear, concise purpose statement isn't enough. What matters is centering our lives around the *right* purpose. Chapter 2 shuttles you into Scripture for *God's* input on the issue of a life purpose. You'll digest verses that will help you formulate a proper purpose statement for your life. The goal of this chapter is to introduce the concept of a personal life purpose statement and to whet your appetite for God's perspective on the matter.

Advantage Plus

Why should you crystallize a Christ-centered purpose statement for your life? Is carving out a purpose statement just religious busywork? Is it just another monotonous, filling-in-the-blank type of exercise? Is the process just a theoretical, cerebral activity that's far removed from the nuts-and-bolts of daily responsibilities?

No. If you complete the next chapter as prescribed, here are some of the advantages you'll experience in the years ahead.

- *Significance, not just success.* In the world's eyes, a successful person is someone who reaches his goals. The athlete who wins an Olympic medal. The student who earns her Ph.D. The entrepreneur who presides over a multimillion dollar company. But from God's perspective the crux of the matter is not whether you reach your goals. *His concern is that you strive for the right goals!* In the week that follows, God's Word will expose you to the *right* goals and elevate eternal values over temporal matters. You'll discover significance to your daily routine, whether or not you succeed on an earthly plane.

- *Meaning, not monotony.* Someone once said, "More people spend their time preparing for something in the future than living to the hilt in the present." But you will discover that nobody has more of a reason

to get up in the morning than a Christian.
What is more meaningful than cultivating
intimacy with the Creator of the universe?
What is more stimulating than serving Him
with our resources and abilities? No one in
the will of God leads a boring existence.
You will grasp the fact that everything we
do in the here and now has eternal consequences.

- *Joy, not just happiness.* Happiness depends
  on happenings. But Stuart Briscoe told an
  audience of believers, "When your happenings don't happen the way you happen to
  want your happenings to happen, *you can
  still be joyful.*"[4] One of Jesus' goals for His
  followers is "that your joy may be made
  full" (John 15:11).

    Making a temporal pursuit the guiding
  mechanism of your life may provide tem-
  porary pleasure, but never joy. A billionaire
  oil magnate was so uptight about losing his
  wealth that he installed a pay telephone in
  his mansion for overnight guests. To save
  on electricity, he replaced all the 100-watt
  light bulbs in his house with the 60-watt variety. He died wealthier, all right. And mis-
  erable.[5]

- *Guidance, not confusion.* A purpose statement for your life will provide an overarching framework within which all decisions
  fit. It will serve as a reference point to help

you plan the future. Want to find a spouse? Decide between two job offers? Map out a financial budget? The weight of these decisions will get lighter when you view the alternatives in light of biblical guidelines and values. You will determine the extent to which each option impedes or accelerates fulfillment of your life objective.

Q Which of the four advantages of a purpose statement is most real in your current experience?

A _____
_____
_____
_____
_____
_____

Go back and put a check mark by it. Thank the Lord for the degree of significance, meaning, joy or guidance He has already provided.

Q Which of the four advantages of a sound life purpose is most lacking in your current experience? Why do you think that's the case?

A _____
_____
_____

Memorable Achievements

Digesting God's Word is integral to discipleship because of all the benefits it provides. So starting with Chapter 2, you'll receive a Bible memory verse that crystallizes the truth of what this discipleship book is all about. Since hiding God's Word in your heart will empower you to apply the concepts you encounter from week to week, make the memory work a top-shelf priority as you proceed through the course.

To underscore its importance, look up the following verses. Jot down the benefit each mentions for memorizing and meditating on Scripture.

• Psalm 119:9-11

_____

• First Peter 1:23

_____

• First Peter 2:2

_____

• Psalm 119:50, 92

_____

• Psalm 119:24, 98-100

_____

• Romans 12:2

_____

Q Which of the benefits of memorizing and meditating on Scripture have you already experienced? Describe a time when you experienced an advantage of hiding Scripture in your heart.

A _____

_____

_____

_____

Q Which benefit of Bible memory are you most eager to experience in the future? Why?

A _____

_____

_____

Many people think they can't memorize Scripture, but here's the truth of the matter: Most people do not lack ability to remember something, they just don't know *how* to memorize a Bible verse so they *can* remember it. What follows are eight tips that will accelerate your memory work. The first letters of each key word form an acrostic: **REMEMBER.**

RESERVE: Reserve a brief chunk of time each day for Scripture memory. Strive for the same time slot every day and view those minutes as an appointment with the Lord.

ENTREAT: To "entreat" means to make a request. Ask the Lord to illumine your thinking about the memory verse. To clarify its meaning. To help you spot every important truth it contains. Display a dependence on the Lord similar to the psalmist's: "Open my eyes, that I may behold wonderful things from Your law" (Psalm 119:18).

MINIMIZE: Memorize just one phrase at a time. Minimizing the amount you cover at any one instance makes the overall task seem less formidable. Concentrating on bite-sized chunks also enables you to learn the verse perfectly, ensuring an accurate rendering in your memory bank.

ENLIST: Enlist a Christian brother or sister to hold you accountable for your memory work. Whether face-to-face or over the phone, ask this person to use the same translation and check for accuracy. Perhaps he or she will join you in the memory exercises!

MEDITATE: Let it penetrate your heart as well as your head. Ask the Lord to encourage or to convict you as necessary. Mull over its practical implications for your life.

BEGIN: Begin your memory work early in the week, as well as early in the day. Starting early gives the Holy Spirit fuel to work with as you proceed with your daily and weekly routine. You will have more opportunities to review the verse and greater likelihood of linking the verse's message to the circumstances of life.

EXPRESS: When we learn something from the Bible, let us express it to others so they too can benefit from it. Tell family members and friends how each verse ministers to you. Look for people who also need the perspective or encouragement the verse offers.

REVIEW: The only way to shuttle Bible verse content from short-term to long-term memory is with persistent review. Going over a verse daily for a while ensures that you will know it three months later, not just three days from now.

Teachable Spirit

What will expedite your successful completion of this *Knowing God* course? An appetite for learning. A heart-felt sense of need for spiritual growth. An openness to God's truth. A realization that you have not arrived, spiritually speaking—that there's more to Christianity than you are currently experiencing. Put simply, the password to a life-changing encounter with God is *teachability*.

Right now, ask the Lord to cultivate within you a teachable spirit. Tell Him that you want this *Knowing God* course to *form* you, not just inform you.

What makes life worth-while is having a big enough objective, something which catches our imagination and lays hold of our allegiance; and this the Christian has, in a way that no other man has. For what higher, more exalted, and more impelling goal can there be than to know God? [1]

—J.I. Packer

Identifying Your Life Purpose

Go to a graveyard outside Lincoln, Kansas and you will see an unusual group of gravestones. They were erected by a man named Davis. When you delve into his personal history, you discover that he began working as a lowly hired hand. Over the years, though, by sheer determination and extreme frugality, he amassed a wallet-bulging fortune. You also find out that Mr. Davis' preoccupation with wealth resulted in a neglect of people. Apparently he had few friends. He was even emotionally distant from his wife's family, who felt that she had married beneath her dignity. Their attitude embittered him. He vowed never to leave his relatives a penny.

When his wife died, Davis hired a sculptor to design an elaborate monument in her memory. The monument consisted of a love seat showing Mr. Davis and his wife sitting together. The result so pleased him that he paid for another showing him kneeling at his wife's grave, placing a wreath on it. That was followed by a third monument— showing his wife kneeling at his future grave site. His monument-building binge continued until he'd spent more than a quarter of a million dollars!

He was often approached about contributing financial aid to worthwhile projects in the town or church, but he rarely gave to them. Most of his small fortune was invested in gravestones. At ninety-two, Mr. Davis died—a sour-hearted resident of the poorhouse.

Decades later, as you saunter through the graveyard, you notice an ironic fact: each monument he commissioned is slowly sinking into the Kansas soil, a victim of neglect, vandalism and time. Inevitably, these temporal objects will follow him into the grave.[2]

Q How does Mr. Davis' story relate to the theme of the previous chapter?

A _____

_____

_____

_____

Q Read Proverbs 28:19. Why was Mr. Davis' preoccupation with gravestones "empty pursuits"?

A _____

_____

_____

_____

You probably noted a parallel between Mr. Davis and the Britisher mentioned at the start of Chapter 1. The British aristocrat's preoccupation with spotted mice was definitely an "empty pursuit." Both Mr. Davis and the Britisher spent their time, energy and material resources for a temporal, rather than eternal, investment. They didn't fit God into their plans, or rather they did not fit themselves into God's plans. As a result, their pursuits were eternally fruitless.

In Chapter 1 you were introduced to the concept of a written purpose statement for your life. You discovered that identifying your current purpose involves analysis of behavior over a period of time. What one *does*—not what one says—reveals his objectives. You reviewed the past year—your decisions, relationships, financial expenditures, etc.—and jotted down what appears to be your reason for existing. You discovered that the life purpose of a Christian should be shaped by Scripture, not the values of culture. And you read four advantages of formulating a biblically informed purpose statement.

Now the spotlight shifts to the Bible, where you will uncover God's agenda for His people. The input you receive will help you revise your purpose statement from Chapter 1 based on a behavioral analysis of the past year. Now you will craft a new personal mission statement that is compatible with eternal values.

Ready to proceed?

A Biblical Perspective

Read the following verses and answer the questions below.

Q 1. Genesis 5:21-24 and Hebrews 11:5. **What compliment did the authors of Genesis and Hebrews pay Enoch?**

A _____

_____

_____

Q 2. Isaiah 43:7. **According to this verse, why were you created?**

A _____

_____

_____

Q 3. Jeremiah 9:23. **What vain pursuits or false goals did Jeremiah cite?**

A _____

_____

_____

Q 4. Jeremiah 9:24. In one sentence, state what Jeremiah considered a worthy pursuit.

A _____

_____

_____

Q 5. John 17:4. What was Jesus' ultimate purpose during His earthly life?

A _____

_____

_____

Q 6. Second Corinthians 5:9. What words from this verse reveal Paul's primary ambition?

A _____

_____

_____

Comparatively Speaking

Ponder the content of the various verses you examined. Let their cumulative effect soak into your mind. The biblical writers employed different terminology. The phrases you probably spotted included:

- "Enoch walked with God" (Genesis 5:24).

- "He was pleasing to God" (Hebrews 11:5).

- "Whom I have created for My glory" (Isaiah 43:7).

- "Boast of this, that he understands and knows Me" (Jeremiah 9:24).

- "I glorified You on the earth" (John 17:4).

- "We have as our ambition . . . to be pleasing to Him" (2 Corinthians 5:9).

You uncovered the life purpose of Enoch, Jesus and Paul. You identified God's desire for mankind through the pens of Isaiah and Jeremiah. Yet a single focus—one unifying passion—stitches together all six Bible passages.

Q In twenty-five words or less, write a "reason for human existence" that is compatible with the above Bible verses.

A _____
_____
_____
_____
_____

Q Remember the purpose statement you wrote back in Chapter 1, the one based on your behavior patterns over the past year? **To what extent is your personal statement consistent with the emphasis in God's Word? What is the Lord saying to you right now regarding the issue of your life's purpose and direction?**

A _____

_____

_____

_____

_____

_____

_____

   Imagine: You were created to enjoy intimacy with the Creator of the universe! To honor Him. To give Him pleasure in the way you operate from day to day. The late missionary martyr Jim Elliot knew what it was like to be preoccupied with God. He wrote: "God, I pray Thee, light these idle sticks of my life and may I burn up for Thee. Consume my life, my God, for it is Yours. I seek not long life, but a full one, like You, Lord Jesus."[3]

Q If God were to "consume your life"—if glorifying and pleasing Him were your number one priority each day—what specific changes would have to occur in your life? How different would your schedule look? Prayerfully record your thoughts.

A _____

_____

_____

_____

_____

Ask the Lord to make *His* purpose and vision become yours. Ask Him to show you the necessary adjustments you need to make in order to live compatibly with it.

The purpose statement you gathered from the various Bible passages probably reads similar to the one below. If it's a life purpose you honestly want to pursue, sign your name below it.

The purpose of my existence is to bring glory to God and to live a life that brings Him pleasure. No matter what the cost, I want to make that my ultimate purpose in life.

_____

(your name)

Memorizing Scripture

Your first memory verse for this discipleship course summarizes the purpose statement you crafted from Scripture: Philippians 4:20. Be ready to recite this verse when you arrive at the next group meeting. Memorize it from a translation rather than a paraphrase.

From Purpose to Process

Right now, your personal mission statement probably seems pretty generic, or broad in scope. That is the nature of purpose statements, whether they are put together by individuals or organizations. A written purpose needs to be specific enough to provide direction, yet general enough to affect every single sphere of living.

The rest of *Knowing God* will help you more fully understand and appreciate this Christ-centered purpose statement. Chapters 3-12 reveal the process that is involved in fleshing it out. Your participation in the weekly discipleship group will refine the concepts and provide a supportive atmosphere for their application. Experiencing that process will take a lifetime, but this discipleship book and the related group discussions will at least nudge you in the right direction.

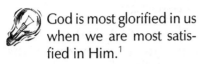 God is most glorified in us when we are most satisfied in Him.[1]

—John Piper

Loving God

The first two chapters provided grist for your thinking in relation to a "life purpose." Your study of Scripture solidified your ultimate objective on planet Earth: *to bring glory to God and to live a life that brings Him pleasure.* As God's child, you exist for His sake. He doesn't exist for yours.

You may be wondering, "How does a person glorify God? What has to happen in order to achieve this biblical purpose?" Mark 12:28-30 answers those questions. It tells of a man who came to Jesus and asked Him what was God's greatest commandment or desire. Jesus' answer is simple yet profound. *To love God with all one's heart, soul, mind and strength.* A life that honors Him and brings Him pleasure stems from a love relationship with Him. Unless we love Him, glorifying Him will not happen.

Since loving Him is integral to glorifying Him, this chapter zeroes in on this question: *How does one's love for God express itself?*

Practicing His Presence

The Practice of the Presence of God is a devotional classic featuring a man who went by the name "Brother Lawrence." The following excerpt from the book shows how he manifested his love for the Lord.

He had resolved to make loving God the purpose of everything he did. This way of living gave him every reason to be satisfied. He said he was glad even to pick up a straw from the ground if he could do it to show his love to God. That kind of love seeks God only—that and nothing else, not even His gifts.

Brother Lawrence told how to form the habit of talking with God all the time, referring all we do to Him. The secret: Ask God in a spirit of genuine diligence. After a little care and after a little time, we will discover His love excites us to continual conversation with God with no difficulty. Actually, for Brother Lawrence, the set times for prayer were no different than other times. He did, of course, retire to pray at the times set by his superior but he did not ask for these set times—nor particularly want them—because his busiest and biggest work assignments did not divert him from God.

He knew fully his call to love God in everything he did, and this he tried faithfully to do. Brother Lawrence confessed his praying was nothing but a sense of the presence of God, his soul being unaware of anything but God's love. When the appointed times of prayer were past, he found no difference, because he went right on with God praising and blessing Him with all his might, so that he lived his life with continual joy.

Again, we ought not to be weary of doing little things for the love of God, who really doesn't think about the greatness of what we do, but the love with which it is performed! If at first we often fail to do everything for the love of God, never mind; the new habit will be formed before long. And once that habit is fixed, certain acts are bound to follow naturally, and to our great delight.[2]

Q What challenges you most about Brother Lawrence's life? Why?

A _____

_____

_____

_____

 Go back and underline one or two sentences from the book that impress you most.

Notice the following phrases from the book excerpt:

- "to make loving God the purpose of everything he did."
- "the habit of talking with God all the time, referring all we do to Him."
- "His love excites us to continual conversation with God."

- "the set times for prayer were no different than other times."
- "his busiest and biggest work assignments did not divert him from God."
- "his call to love God in everything he did."
- "do everything for the love of God."

Clearly, Brother Lawrence modeled a significant principle for us: *loving God occurs in the smallest details of daily life.* When we are truly in love with Him, we maintain a God-consciousness throughout the day. Everything we do becomes an occasion for showing Him our love and bringing Him glory.

Unfortunately, many Christians find it difficult to fellowship with God throughout the day. Their responsibilities distract them so much that they can go through an entire day without even thinking of Jesus. These responsibilities may even be "spiritual," like going to church, yet the Christian is so caught up in his *routine for* Jesus that he forgets his *relationship with* Jesus.

Fellowship with the Lord, like any intimate relationship, is what is most important in life. It is the priority which cannot be displaced by any other responsibility. To experience fellowship with God, you must give Him your attention, not just on Sunday mornings, but every day, all day.

You may be thinking that "practicing the presence of God" is easier said than done. You are correct—it *is* challenging, particularly in the hectic pace of modern life. Yet fellowship with God is possible throughout the day.

Focusing Your Attention

The concept of expressing your love for God by "practicing His presence" all day long may intrigue you. The question in your mind is, "But how?" Here are concrete suggestions to better focus your attention on Him.

- *Meditate.* Focus attention on Him throughout the day by meditating on the Bible verses you've been memorizing or a passage you have been reading. To meditate means to think about how something may apply to yourself or to your situation. If you read a chapter in the morning, ponder its implications for your decisions, relationships and responsibilities as you proceed through the day. If your Bible reading extolled the value of faith, keep asking yourself, "How can my trust in the Lord reveal itself in this business decision? In this dilemma regarding my child? What attributes of God make Him worthy of my trust?" Don't stop short by simply thinking about God's Word. Use that as a springboard to think about God Himself.

Read Psalm 1:2. **Identify various times, both during the day and at night, when you can think about God and His Word.**

A _____

• *Talk.* Converse with the Lord about the people and circumstances you face throughout the day. Your concerns don't have to be audible. The Lord hears the thoughts you send His way, not just your words. As you walk into that board meeting, whisper in your mind, "Father, help me to trust You with the decision they make today." Or "Enable me to express myself clearly as I make the proposal." Practice carrying on two conversations at once: one directed toward God, the other toward man.

Q Read First Thessalonians 5:17. **Describe a specific scenario from your home life or work in which you talked to God while fulfilling another responsibility.**

A _____

- **Thank.** Express gratitude to the Lord for taken-for-granted blessings, plus positive experiences during the day. Notice these concrete examples: "I'm grateful my car has lasted so long. I appreciate the guidance you gave when I purchased it years ago." "Lord, thank You for a husband who still kisses me before he leaves for work." "Thanks for bringing an efficient and sensitive tutor for our son." Psalm 100:4-5 reads, "Give thanks to Him; bless His name. For the LORD is good; His lovingkindness is everlasting and His faithfulness to all generations." Constantly giving God thanks throughout the day keeps your attention focused on Him.

Q In what sense is gratitude a way of expressing love to someone?

A _____

_____

_____

_____

- **Look.** Look for evidence of God at work as you proceed through the day. Examples include answers to prayer, instances of unusual timing or arrangement of circumstances that smooth the way for you, obvious maturing in a young Christian you know, or indications of fruitfulness in some ministry you (or someone you know) have exercised. David Mains encourages believers to go on a "God hunt" to keep an eye out for divine activity in the routine events of each day.[3]

Q Read Psalm 145:1-2. **When you see evidence of God at work in your life, how does it affect your attitude toward Him?**

A _____

_____

_____

_____

_____

- *Tell.* Another way to cultivate a God-consciousness is to tell others in your sphere of influence what you are learning and experiencing spiritually. Share a verse or truth from your Bible reading that encouraged you. Pass along an insight you gleaned from your pastor's last sermon. Ask a believing friend to pray for you about a particular problem. Inform someone of an answered prayer or incident revealing God's faithfulness. Verbalizing aspects of your spiritual walk increases sensitivity to His work in your life.

Q Read Psalm 145:6-7. **What words or phrases from these verses encourage you to talk to others about the Lord?**

A _____

_____

_____

_____

_____

Q List one thing from your study or spiritual experience that you can tell someone this week.

A _____

_____

_____

_____

- *Sing.* When possible, sing or hum a favorite Christian chorus or hymn. The lyrics will remind you of His attributes and past deeds or sustain you during discouraging moments. "Serve the LORD with gladness; come before Him with joyful singing" (Psalm 100:2). Think of a couple of choruses or hymns that encourage your worship of God. Obtain a copy of their lyrics and carry the words with you until you have memorized them. Singing to God, and not just about Him, keeps you in His presence.

Q Which of these six tips for focusing attention on God do you most often practice? How has this been an expression of your love for the Lord?

A _____

_____

_____

_____

Q In order to better demonstrate your love for Him, which suggestion for "practicing the presence of God" do you need to implement more often?

A _____

_____

_____

_____

Psalm 73:25 says, "Whom have I in heaven but You? And besides You, I desire nothing on earth." Like the psalmist, long to live in God's presence throughout the day. Break out of the mind-set that God only wants your attention on Sundays or during designated prayer times. He created you to have a love relationship with Him. One that is characterized by intimacy throughout your daily routine. Don't feel that you always have to do something to be in His presence. More often than not, you may just want to be still and bask in His love for you. The point is God has your attention.

First Corinthians 1:9 says, "God is faithful, through whom you were called into fellowship with His Son, Jesus Christ our Lord." Long for God's company. Be satisfied with nothing less than moment by moment fellowship with Him.

Memorizing Scripture

Begin practicing the presence of God. At the next discipleship group meeting, be ready to give a report on how well you focused your attention on God throughout the day. Also, memorize Mark 12:30 before next week. This verse reminds you that loving God is your top-shelf priority.

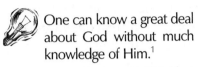 One can know a great deal about God without much knowledge of Him.[1]

—J.I. Packer

Knowing God

How can you tell when you're really in love with another person? What distinguishes genuine love from infatuation?

When you experience the real thing, certain characteristics describe your relationship. As you read these characteristics, think of the time you first fell in love. When you are in love:

- You spend time together and it goes by quickly. Hours seem to turn into minutes.

- You miss each other when separated and long to be together again.

- You rearrange your schedule to make yourself available for the other person.

- You relate everything about you to the one you love. You want the way you talk, look and act to please your loved one.

- You give extravagantly. There are no limits to your gifts.

- Spending time together is not burden-some. You do not have to be coaxed into giving your beloved your time.

- You find fulfillment in the other's pres-ence. It does not matter what you do or don't do as long as you are together.

- You talk about everything but also enjoy just being quiet together.

- You like to be alone with that person as often as possible.

- Your loved one has no competition for your affection.

- You may appear foolish to others when with your loved one because you are oblivious to anything else around you.

- You read his/her love notes over and over.[2]

A person's love for Jesus Christ shows in similar ways. Take inventory for a moment. Exercise gut-wrenching honesty and evaluate your relationship with the Lord.

 Go back and put a check mark by those characteristics that definitely describe your "love life" with Jesus Christ. (Don't check an item unless there's concrete evidence of its authenticity.) **Then put a question mark by the characteristics that do not usually de-scribe your personal relationship with Christ.**

Q Now mull over the items you checked and questioned. **To what extent do you love Jesus Christ? What conclusions can you draw from this evaluative exercise?**

A _____

_____

_____

_____

_____

Chapter 2 acquainted you with life's ultimate purpose: *to bring glory and pleasure to God.* Chapter 3 showed that you glorify Him only when you are in love with Him. You discovered that loving Him involves cultivating a constant God-consciousness, or learning to "practice His presence" as you proceed through the routines of work and human relationships. Now it is time for you to pause and reflect. How can a person tell whether or not he really loves God? If a person senses that his love for the Lord is shallow or deficient, how can he deepen that love?

Here's the "bottom line." *Growing in love with someone is a process that's accelerated as you get to know the person better. The better you get to know Him, the more your love for God intensifies.* So "evaluating your love life" with Jesus Christ amounts to evaluating the extent to which you know Him. That is why this chapter will confront you with these questions: *Do I actually know the Lord, or am I relying on knowledge about Him to get by spiritually? Have I been introduced to Christianity without having been introduced to Christ as a Person? Once I enter into a relationship with Christ, what are the positive consequences of growing in my love for Him?*

In other words, before delving into chapters about deepening your relationship with the Lord, let's step back and make sure the relationship exists. What you learn may lead to the conclusion that you don't really know Him at all. If you're confident your relationship with God *is* genuine, you'll identify the value of growing increasingly closer to Him.

Evidences of a Relationship with God

According to Jeremiah, knowing God personally is the only valid reason for boasting.

> Thus says the LORD, "Let not a wise man boast of his wisdom, and let not the mighty man boast of his might, let not a rich man boast of his riches; but let him who boasts boast of this, that he understands and knows Me." (Jeremiah 9:23-24)

Yet as already suggested, *knowing Him* isn't the same as *knowing about Him*. You *know about* the President of the United States and sports personalities who earn millions every year. But chances are you don't really know them on a personal level. When it comes to your relationship with Jesus, be sure you don't merely know some facts about Him. Be sure you have been introduced to Him and have an ongoing relationship with Him. Whether or not you know the Lord personally has eternal consequences. As John 17:3 indicates, "This is eternal life, that they may know You, the only true God, and Jesus Christ whom You have sent."

God's Word unveils characteristics of persons who have eternal life—who know the Lord instead of just knowing about Him. Look up the following passages in First John. Then list in sentence form several evidences of an authentic relationship with Jesus Christ. What you find will either expose your need of a relationship with Him, or provide faith-boosting assurance of the relationship's validity.

First John 2:3-6; 3:14, 19-24; 5:4-5

_____

_____

_____

_____

_____

_____

_____

_____

Steps to Knowing God Personally

Has this chapter's content planted a seed of doubt in your mind? Are you unsure about your relationship with Christ? Perhaps a review of basic biblical truth is in order. If you yearn for a life-changing introduction to Jesus Christ, proceed through the following steps.

1. *Admit your need for a "saving" relationship with Christ.*

   The biblical term "salvation" means "deliverance." It suggests that we're facing some type of danger and need to be snatched away and brought to a place of safety. The Old Testament concept of salvation often refers to Israel's deliverance from an enemy nation. When we apply the term to Christian experience, we have a different kind of deliverance in mind.

   Q a. Read Jeremiah 17:9, Mark 7:14-23 and Romans 3:10-12, 23. **Why does every human being need deliverance?**

   A _____

   _____

   _____

   Ever since the first couple, Adam and Eve, disobeyed God, a cut-off-from-God state has been passed down to all mankind (Romans 5:12).

   Q b. Digest First Peter 1:15-16. **What is there about God that makes it impossible for Him to have fellowship with sinful human beings?**

   A _____

   _____

   _____

   _____

Q c. God's Word insists that we have a natural bent for going our own way (called a "sinful nature"). Now read Romans 5:12 and 6:23. **What is the ultimate consequence of sin?**

A _____

_____

_____

Admitting your need for a saving relationship with Christ involves **confessing** your sin. The verb "confess" means "to say the same thing." Confessing sins means we agree with God about them. We start seeing sins through His eyes, so to speak, and realize that they separate us from fellowship with Him.

2. *Believe in God's provision for an eternal relationship with Him.*

So far we've concluded that we need deliverance from sin and its penalty. Yet we're unable to deliver ourselves from this dilemma. Sounds bleak, doesn't it? Except God took the initiative and dealt a knockout punch to the sin problem.

Q Look up the following Bible passages. Review what God did on our behalf in order to make a relationship with Him possible. **What distinctive aspects of God's salvation do you find in each scripture? After each reference, summarize its truth in your own**

words. Jot down something distinctive in each passage about God's provision of salvation.

a. Romans 5:6-11

A _____

_____

_____

_____

b. First John 4:9-10

A _____

_____

_____

_____

c. Ephesians 2:8-9

A _____

_____

_____

_____

d. Isaiah 53:4-6

A _____

_____

_____

_____

e. Second Corinthians 5:21

A _____

_____

_____

_____

_____

From the cross, Jesus cried out, "It is finished!" (John 19:30). The Greek word translated "finished" was found on a bill of debt dating back to the first century. The final payment on the debt had been paid. This word, meaning, "paid in full," was boldly printed across the piece of paper, which then served as a receipt. What a relief! Jesus was saying that the debt of sin would be "paid in full" by His death on the cross. What a Savior!

3. *Respond to the Holy Spirit's work in your heart by accepting His offer of an intimate relationship with Him.*

The fact that Jesus took the penalty for sin does *not* mean everyone is automatically saved. Every individual needs to respond to the Holy Spirit's wooing by turning to God. Whoever feels convicted of sin and believes in the Lord's provision on the cross needs to consciously accept His offer of eternal life. The verses that follow tell what's involved in accepting His offer of a relationship.

Q How do these verses describe the experience? John 1:11-12; Romans 10:9-10; Revelation 3:20.

A _____

_____

_____

_____

Have you responded to Jesus Christ in this way? "Knowing God" necessarily involves probing to determine if you've ever been introduced to Him in the first place. If you've identified yourself as one who has **known about Him** without **knowing Him,** make the following prayer your own.

> *Jesus, I acknowledge my need for a relationship with You. I admit I'm a sinner by nature, and my sin separates me from You. But I also believe You paid the death penalty that I deserve. Your death on the cross makes forgiveness and eternal life possible. I want to know You personally, not just know about You. I want to live a life that pleases You and to grow in my love for You. So by faith, I invite You into my heart so You can change me into the person You want me to be. Thank You, Jesus.*

If you prayed those thoughts today, write your name and the date in the space below.

> *Today, I accepted Jesus Christ's offer of eternal life and entered a life-changing relationship with Him. Now that I know*

*Him personally, I can launch the lifelong
process of deepening my love for Him by
learning more and more about Him.*

_____

(name)

_____

(date)

Benefits of Knowing God More Intimately

If this review of biblical truth convinced you that you already know the Lord, pause right now and thank Him for His provision of salvation. Ask Him to fan the flames of the love you already have for Him. As you get to know Him more intimately, you'll experience a number of benefits to an increasing degree.

In a discourse to His disciples, Jesus pointed out the values of knowing God better and better. He used the term "abide" (or "remain") to describe the closeness of a growing relationship with Him.

Q Read John 15:1-11. What are the values, or benefits, of intimacy with the Lord that He mentions?

A _____

_____

_____

_____

Q Which result of an abiding relationship is most evident in your life right now? (Thank Him for this consequence of knowing Him.)

A _____

_____

_____

Q Which result of an intimate relationship is most lacking in your life? (Tell Him you want greater intimacy so you can experience all the values of knowing Him.)

A _____

_____

_____

While you're mulling over the values of knowing Christ intimately, digest the following words from Robertson McQuilkin. Note how the benefits he cites parallel the content of John 15:1-11: "To know Him is to trust Him in a personal relationship. To know Him is to obey Him in growing into His likeness. But above all to know Him is to love Him, to companion with Him so that all of life's joys are shared joys, all of life's problems are a great opportunity to put His power on display."[3]

Memorizing Scripture

Before your group meets, memorize Philippians 3:8. Note how Paul's burning ambition was to know Christ more intimately. And note how everything else paled in comparison to His intimacy with the Lord.

Don't Keep Him to Yourself

You've determined whether you know God personally or just know *about* Him. You've identified the values of knowing Him intimately, cited by Jesus Christ Himself. Now it's time to turn your attention to people you know who don't know Him. How can you help others experience the benefits you enjoy as a result of knowing Christ? That's the question tackled in Chapter 5.

I have found that my own spiritual life is usually much healthier when I am in the midst of some evangelistic endeavor. Now that is a confession, I know, of my own spiritual fickleness. But it is also a revelation, I believe, of a spiritual law. As I see people coming to Christ, I relive vicariously my own spiritual birth. It is a renewing catharsis. The Christian church and the Christian person remain healthy only as one hand is stretched up to receive from God while the other is stretched out to share with man.[1]

—Leighton Ford

CHAPTER FIVE

Helping Others to Know God

The Dead Sea is a lake occupying the southern end of the Jordan River Valley. Its northern tip rests not far from the city of Jerusalem. This sheet of greenish, salty water is eleven miles across at its widest point and almost fifty miles long. The water itself is marked by a distinctively bitter taste and a nauseous smell.

Have you ever wondered why it is called the "Dead" Sea? The water is so intensely saline and contains so many minerals such as bromide and sulfur that few living things can survive in it. The water houses these minerals and cannot support many life forms like a normal lake for one basic reason: *The Dead Sea has inlets, but no outlets.* Millions of tons of water—from the Jordan and several smaller streams—flow into the basin daily. But no streams flow from it to other parts of the country. This salty sea would be fresh or only mildly saline had it an outlet, but the landlocked basin in which it rests in that hot and arid climate serves as a gigantic evaporating pan. Flooding is prevented because the dry heat rapidly evaporates the water.

This fact about the Dead Sea reflects a truth of Christian living: *We need to construct outlets so that whatever blessings flow into our lives eventually refresh others as well.* Our lives aren't as fresh, reproductive and vibrant if what we're learning and experiencing is not channeled toward others with whom we have contact.

The focus of this book is your own relationship with God. You've determined that glorifying Him is life's ultimate purpose (Chapters 1 and 2). You discovered that you glorify Him when you're in love with Him. Loving Him involves cultivating a constant God-consciousness, or "practicing His presence" as you proceed through daily routines (Chapter 3). Loving Him depends on, and is intensified by, knowing Him ever more intimately. So you evaluated whether you know God personally or you just know *about* Him. You reviewed how to enter a saving relationship with Him and the benefits of knowing Him more intimately as you progress in the faith (Chapter 4).

Now the focus shifts to your role in helping others to know Him. As suggested by the Dead Sea analogy, you have the privilege of taking the reservoir of experience you have with Him and constructing outlets so others can enter a relationship with Him. If you keep your knowledge of Jesus to yourself, the result will be stagnation. If you become a channel though which eternal life can flow to others, your own relationship with Him will be marked by vitality. (Besides, the more important Jesus is to you, the more you'll want others to experience the benefits of knowing Him.)

A Strategy for Introducing Christ

Telling others about Him requires an awareness of key Bible truths, plus a practical method for conveying those truths. In Chapter 4, in a section labeled "Steps to Knowing God Personally," you examined basic content in what is often called the "plan of salvation."

The main thrust of this chapter is to give you a practical method for helping others get to know Him. You'll learn to use one verse—John 3:16—to convey the basic truths you reviewed in Chapter 4. *View this "one-verse method" as the tool you need to start constructing those outlets for the blessings you've received.*

What follows is a step-by-step explanation, including diagrams, for using John 3:16 in personal evangelism.

INTRODUCTION

TRANSITION: Say that John 3:16 is the most famous verse in the entire Bible and that you want to show this person why.

ACTION: Take out a piece of paper and write the words of John 3:16 at the very top of the page in this particular order, leaving room on the page for subsequent steps. (To help you remember this order, note that the middle two phrases both start with the word "that" and both end with a reference to Jesus Christ.) Number these phrases in the following order: 1, 3, 4, 2. (See Step 1.)

John 3:16

1. For "God" so "love"d the "world,"
3. that He gave His only begotten Son,
4. that whoever believes in Him
2. should not perish, but have eternal life.

Step 1: Introduction

EXPLANATION: The reason John 3:16 is so famous is because it summarizes the Bible in four spiritual truths. If you understand these four spiritual truths, you will understand what the entire Bible is all about.

GOD'S PURPOSE

TRANSITION: Let's look at the first truth.

ACTION: Put quotation marks around the words "God," "love," and "world." Then about halfway down the page, diagram this truth by writing the word

"God" on the right, the word "world" on the left, and the word "love" down the middle. (See Step 2.)

EXPLANATION: God created man to have a personal relationship with Him. He wants this relationship to be one of love, one where God shows His love to people and where people show their love to Him.

John 3:16

1. For "God" so "loved" the "world,"
3. that He gave His only begotten Son,
4. that whoever believes in Him
2. should not perish, but have eternal life.

WORLD   L   GOD
                            O
                            V
                            E

Step 2: God's Purpose

TRANSITION: Why do you think that more people are not experiencing this loving personal relationship?

ACTION: Write the word "sin" below the word "love." Then draw two cliffs, one under the word "world," and the other under the word "God." (See Step 3.)

EXPLANATION: It is because of sin. Sin is disobeying God. When someone is offended it causes problems in the relationship. Sin causes a separation between God and man.

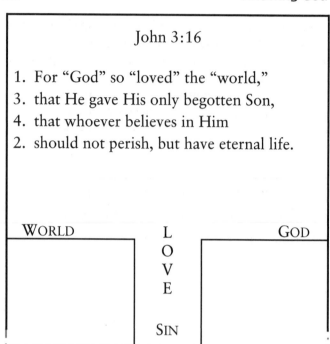

John 3:16

1. For "God" so "loved" the "world,"
3. that He gave His only begotten Son,
4. that whoever believes in Him
2. should not perish, but have eternal life.

WORLD   L   GOD
                         O
                         V
                         E

                        SIN

Step 3

MAN'S PROBLEM

TRANSITION: Let's look at the second spiritual truth. It says, "should not perish, but have eternal life."
ACTION: Put quotation marks around the word "perish" and write it under the left-hand cliff, the one with the word "world" on it. Then draw an arrow downward from the word "perish" and write the word "hell." (See Step 4.)
EXPLANATION: It is bad enough to be separated from God's love, but it gets worse. The Bible says that if anyone dies physically while spiritually separated from God, he will spend eternity in a place called hell.

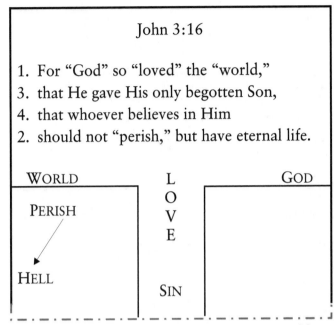

Step 4: Man's Problem

TRANSITION: That's bad news, but this second spiritual truth also gives some good news.

ACTION: Put quotation marks around the word "eternal life" and write them under the right-hand cliff. Draw an arrow downward and write the word "heaven." (See Step 5.)

EXPLANATION: The good news is that God does not want man to spend eternity in hell. His desire is to have a personal relationship with man so that they can live together forever in a place called heaven.

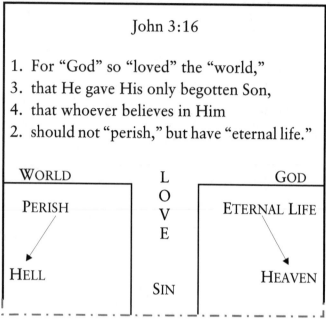

GOD'S REMEDY

TRANSITION: The question then becomes: How does one deal with his problem of sin? That leads us to the third spiritual truth.

ACTION: Put quotation marks around the word "Son" and write it on the diagram so that it shares the letter "O" with the word "love." Then draw a cross that encloses the words "Son" and "love" and bridges the two cliffs. (See Step 6.)

EXPLANATION: God took care of the sin problem by sending His Son, Jesus Christ, to live a perfect life, then die on the cross in order that a person's sin could be forgiven. The amazing thing is that after Jesus was dead and buried, He rose from the dead, proving God has the power to save people from a destiny of torment.

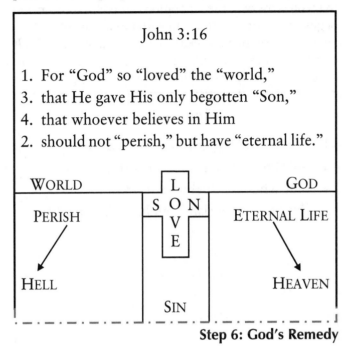

Step 6: God's Remedy

MAN'S RESPONSE

TRANSITION: The question now is, how can a person cross over the bridge that Christ has provided? The fourth spiritual truth gives the answer.

ACTION: Draw an arrow from the word "world" to the word "God." Put quotation marks around the words "believes in Him" and write them on top of the arrow. (See Step 7.)

EXPLANATION: It is not enough to simply know (1) that God loves you, (2) that your sin keeps you from that love and will ultimately send you to hell and (3) that Jesus Christ's death on the cross spares you from it all. It is only as you believe in Christ as your Lord and Savior that you cross over the separation caused by your sin and begin a personal relationship with God. This word "believe" is more than just believing in Abraham Lincoln. It means to commit everything you know about yourself to everything you know about Christ.

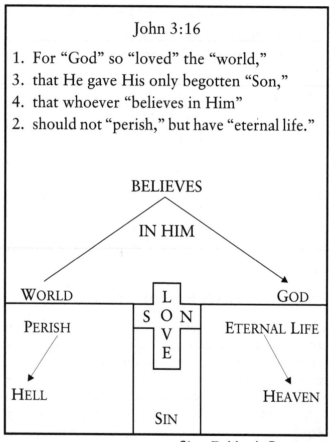

John 3:16

1. For "God" so "loved" the "world,"
3. that He gave His only begotten "Son,"
4. that whoever "believes in Him"
2. should not "perish," but have "eternal life."

BELIEVES

IN HIM

WORLD   GOD

L
S   O   N
    V
    E

PERISH   ETERNAL LIFE

HELL   HEAVEN

SIN

Step 7: Man's Response

INVITATION

TRANSITION: May we personalize this for a moment?
ACTION: On the diagram on the next page, draw a circle around the word "whoever," then write the word "whoever" above the phrase "believes in Him." (See Step 8.)
EXPLANATION: The Bible says whoever believes in Him will cross over to God and receive eternal life. Where would you place yourself on this diagram?

- If they put themselves on the right-hand side, ask them to tell you about when and how they crossed over.

- If they put themselves on the left-hand side, or on top of the cross, ask the next question.

Do you see anything keeping you from placing your faith in Christ and crossing over to God right now?

If they say "yes," ask them what their questions are and deal with them accordingly. If you do not know the answer to a question, tell them you will try to find out.

If they say "no," prepare to lead them in prayer expressing their desire to God.

PRAYER OF SALVATION

TRANSITION: If you desire to place your faith in Christ to make you right with God, it's as easy as 1, 2, 3, 4.
ACTION: Put the number 1 under the right-hand cliff, the number 2 under the left-hand cliff, the number 3 under the cross, and the number 4 beside the word "whoever." (See Step 9.)

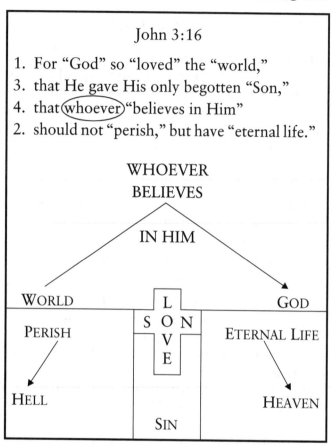

John 3:16

1. For "God" so "loved" the "world,"
3. that He gave His only begotten "Son,"
4. that (whoever) "believes in Him"
2. should not "perish," but have "eternal life."

WHOEVER
BELIEVES

IN HIM

WORLD   GOD

      L
    S O N
PERISH   V   ETERNAL LIFE
      E

HELL   HEAVEN

SIN

Step 8: Invitation

EXPLANATION: If you would like to trust Christ you can do so right now. Tell God: 1) that you are grateful that He loves you; 2) that you are sorry for your sin that has separated you from His love; 3) that you are grateful that He gave His only Son to forgive your sin; and 4) that you believe Christ will make you right with Him right now.

I can pray and you can repeat after me. Remember, what is most important is the attitude of your heart, not the words of your mouth. You can pray the right words, but if your heart is not truly convinced that only Christ can make you right with God, then you will not cross over to God. Let's close our eyes and pray right now. (Pray the above four truths back to God.)

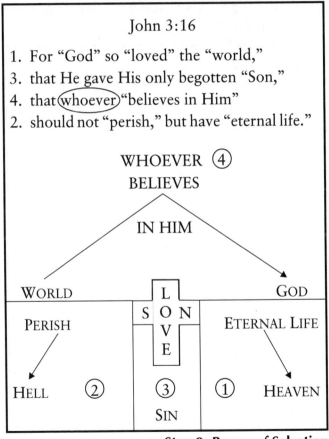

John 3:16

1. For "God" so "loved" the "world,"
3. that He gave His only begotten "Son,"
4. that (whoever) "believes in Him"
2. should not "perish," but have "eternal life."

WHOEVER ④

BELIEVES

IN HIM

WORLD   GOD

PERISH   SON   ETERNAL LIFE

L O V E

HELL ②   ③   ① HEAVEN

SIN

Step 9: Prayer of Salvation

PRACTICING John 3:16

Use the space provided in the box below to practice sharing the message using John 3:16. Do this as much as possible without referring back to the chapter. If you must look back, place a smiley face where you got stuck. These smiley faces will serve as a reminder to you where you need to review in order to enhance your presentation.

Follow Through

1. Present the one-verse method using John 3:16 to two people. They can be close friends, family members, or from the group, if you are going through this book with others.
2. Make notes of what you did best and on what needs more work.
3. Look for opportunities to build friendships or talk to non-Christians.

Memory Verse

Before the next session hide Psalm 73:25 in your heart.

Godliness means responding to God's revelation in trust and obedience, faith and worship, prayer and praise, submission and service. Life must be seen and lived in the light of God's Word. This, and nothing else, is true religion.[1]

—J.I. Packer

Seeking God through His Word

How do other people get to know you? How do they find out your hobbies, your favorite foods and your most cherished memories? How do they become aware of your innermost joys and burdens? Your goals for the future?

Perhaps they uncover a few facts about you from your friends and relatives. Most of their information, though, comes directly from you. They can't get to know you well unless you choose to reveal information about yourself. Your *revelation* of self is the key to others' knowledge of you. The more you're willing to reveal, the more intimately others can know you.

"Revelation" is an important word for Christians. All religions except Christianity began
with a human attempt to discover or to explain
God. But Christianity began with God's attempt to reach humanity! God took the initiative. He decided to create humankind and to
reveal Himself to us for the purpose of enjoying
an ongoing relationship with us. Primarily
through the Bible and the person of Jesus
Christ, God has revealed His nature, His plans,
and His will for Creation. Without His deliber-
ate revelation, we couldn't know what God is
like, what He has done in history, or what He
will do in the future.[2]

In Chapters 1 and 2, you identified the overarching purpose that should serve as the guiding mechanism for your life: to bring glory and pleasure to
God. You discovered that a God-honoring life happens as a result of love for Him—a love you express
by "practicing His presence" throughout the day
(Chapter 3). Since loving God depends on knowing
Him, you evaluated your "love life" by determining
the extent to which you know Him. A Bible study
helped you determine whether you know Him personally through what is called a salvation experience, or if you merely know about Him (Chapter
4). Then in Chapter 5 you discovered a practical
tool for helping others get to know Him.

Whether you just entered a relationship with
the Lord or determined that you already have a
personal relationship, here is the next logical
question: *How do I get to know God better?* Since

knowing Him more intimately will intensify your love for Him and enable you to glorify Him, the issue of how to grow closer to God is a fundamental one for believers.

That is where the next few chapters fit in. You get to know the Lord better *by seeking Him*—choosing to build the relationship by utilizing the means He has provided for intimacy. Seeking Him correctly involves seeking a deeper acquaintance through understanding His words in the Bible (Chapter 6), communicating with Him through prayer (Chapter 7), establishing a daily time alone with God (Chapter 8) and nurturing close relationships with others who know Him (Chapter 9).

As the introduction to this chapter points out, the Bible is God's way of revealing Himself to us. So the process of "seeking God" inevitably draws us to Scripture. Without understanding what He has revealed about Himself, there can't be much of a relationship. In this chapter, you'll identify the benefits of seeking Him in Scripture. And you'll practice a method that maximizes your Bible study time.

"Bottom Line" Benefits

The ultimate consequence of Bible reading is a closer relationship with God. But let's consider more specific benefits that work in tandem to draw you closer to Him. The following verses reveal potential results of delving into Scripture. Jot down at least one reason to read, or result of reading, for each set of references.

Q 1. Luke 24:44-45; John 5:39; 20:30-31

A

Q 2. Jeremiah 15:16; Psalm 19:8

A

Q 3. Second Timothy 3:16-17

A

Q 4. Psalm 119:8, 11

A

Q 5. Psalm 119:28, 50, 52

A _____

_____

_____

_____

Q 6. Psalm 119:24, 98-99

A _____

_____

_____

_____

Q 7. Which benefit of Bible study means most to you right now? Why?

A _____

_____

_____

_____

Q 8. Describe a time when you experienced one of the benefits you identified in the Scripture search. Be specific.

A _____

_____

_____

_____

Q 9. Which positive consequence of Bible reading is most missing from your personal experience? Why do you think that is the case?

A _____

_____

_____

_____

Experiencing those benefits requires effort on your part. Commit to a daily habit of Bible reading. Try setting a definite time of day. Set your alarm fifteen minutes earlier each morning. Or reserve the last few minutes before you turn in at night. Some of us are zombies before 8:00 a.m., but perky at 11:00 p.m. It all depends on how God put you together. What's important is not the time of day but determining a set time. A lady who read her Bible at night said, "If the Lord had intended for me to get up with the sunrise, He would have scheduled it later in the day!"

The specific time of day you will devote to Bible reading is _____.

A Meaningful Method

Whoever seeks the Lord **READS** the Bible. To expedite your Bible exploration, employ the following acrostic.

R = **READ** THE PASSAGE

Strive to read at least a chapter a day. At that pace, you can read the entire New Testament in just nine months. When you select a passage to read, go through the entire section once before giving focused attention to specific verses or details. This allows you to see the "big picture," to see how a particular verse or episode fits into the total context.

If you are relatively new to the Bible, start your reading in the New Testament. It is easier to understand than much of the Old Testament, and it puts the spotlight on the cornerstone of our faith, Jesus Christ. Perhaps the best place to begin is the Gospel of Mark. Mark's narrative reads like a slide presentation of Jesus' life. It is a short, action-packed record of who Jesus is and why He came. On the other hand, if you are familiar with the Bible or have finished reading the New Testament, Psalms is an excellent place to begin the Old Testament. Most psalms are short but powerful. Each one focuses on a person's heart-relationship with God.

E = ENJOY MARKING KEY WORDS/PHRASES

As you read, particular words or phrases will grab your attention. You will view certain items as more important than others, or at least more pertinent to you. When that happens, mark those outstanding words as a reminder to ponder their significance. Your marking may take the form of underlining, circling key words, writing in the margins—you name it!

Here's what one person marked in Psalm 1. He circled key verbs. The boxed in words convey the passage's theme. He employed a dotted line to show analogies. He underlined the result of spending time in God's Word. He drew lines in the left margin to note a key contrast.

1. How **blessed** is the man who does not walk in the counsel of the wicked, nor stand in the path of sinners, nor sit in the seat of scoffers!

2. But his delight is in the law of the LORD, and in His law he meditates day and night.

3. He will be like a tree firmly planted by streams of water, which **yields its fruit in its season, and its leaf does not wither; and in whatever he does, he** prospers.

4. The wicked are not so, but they are like chaff which the wind drives away.

5. Therefore the wicked will not stand in the judgment, nor sinners in the assembly of the righteous.

6. For the LORD knows the way of the righteous, but the way of the wicked will perish.

blessed vs. like chaff

prosperity vs. perish

A = ASK GOD FOR GUIDANCE

Whenever you read, make the psalmist's prayer your own: "Open my eyes, that I may behold wonderful things from Your law" (119:18). The Bible is a book of spiritual truth. It requires the Holy Spirit to take the truth and make it real to your heart. So as you read, ask God to give you understanding so you know what the Bible is talking about and how it applies to you.

D = DETERMINE TIMELESS TRUTHS

To maximize your Bible reading, keep a pen and pad handy. To determine timeless, life-changing truths, jot down impressions, questions and insights that surface as you mull over the text.

Knowing what kinds of information and insights to look for will facilitate your note taking. Use the following questions to prod your thinking. These probes will serve as a crowbar and open up the text for you. You won't find an answer to every question in every chapter you read. Yet employing questions of this sort will always result in more substantive note taking.

- What timeless commands does the passage contain? What are their significance to me?

- What words, phrases or ideas are repeated in the passage? Do these repetitions serve as clues to important truths?

- What contrasts do I see in the text? What point is the author making with these contrasts?

- What actions or attributes of the Lord does the text mention?

- How do persons mentioned in the text serve as either positive or negative examples?

- What attitudes or behaviors is the Lord either recommending or prohibiting in this passage?

Here are a couple of insights we recorded during a study of Psalm 1:

- Psalm 1 *contrasts* the ultimate destinies of the wicked and the righteous person (1:3-6). How I live now will affect the quality of my life in the future.

- We *recommends* daily meditation in God's Word as the basis for a fruitful life (1:2-3).

S = STRIVE FOR DAILY OBEDIENCE

During this last phase of your Bible study, after you have examined what God says and identified timeless truths, then you surrender yourself to His Word's practical implications. You yield to the changes He wants to make in your life as a result of what you just read. You consciously strive to apply the Bible to your life.

To help pinpoint areas for obedience for each passage, finish the following incomplete sentences. Ask the Holy Spirit to use these thought catalysts to expose one application for each passage you read. Then write it down.

- **One reason to thank or to praise the Lord I found in the passage is . . .**

_____

_____

_____

_____

- **One truth or principle that encourages me is . . .**

_____

_____

_____

_____

- **A sin or shortcoming in my life that the passage exposes is . . .**

_____

_____

_____

_____

- **One way the content of this passage should affect my daily life is . . .**

_____

_____

_____

_____

Notice how one person identified an area for obedience and change after examining Psalm 1. Here's what he wrote.

*"Lord Jesus, one shortcoming in my life is the lack
of **meditation** when I read Your Word. I'm too often
in a hurry when I read. The time is often so perfunc-
tory, as if what matters is the act of reading instead
of fellowship with You. Forgive me for not thinking
more about what I read. Remind me that the purpose of it all is to know You better and to please You
more consistently. Amen."*

Reading Practice

Developing Bible study competence is a lot like
learning how to swim. You can't learn how to do
it unless you are *in the water!* Now let's shift from
explanation of the **READS** method to *implement-
ing* it. Ready to dive in?

Use Psalm 27 for your practice run. Read it
through once. Enjoy marking words/phrases that
you perceive as important. Ask God for guidance as
you proceed. Determine timeless truths by taking
notes on the chapter, paying special attention to
commands, repetitions, contrasts, deeds or attributes of God, positive or negative examples and behaviors either recommended or prohibited in the
text. Then strive to obey by identifying one or more
personal applications of the material. (If you are
part of a study group, complete the project before
the next meeting.)

PSALM 27

The LORD is my light and my salvation;
Whom shall I fear?
The LORD is the defense of my life;

Whom shall I dread?
When evildoers came upon me to devour
     my flesh,
My adversaries and my enemies, they
     stumbled and fell.
Though a host encamp against me,
My heart will not fear;
Though war rise against me,
In spite of this I shall be confident.

One thing I have asked from the LORD, that
     I shall seek:
That I may dwell in the house of the LORD
     all the days of my life,
To behold the beauty of the LORD
And to meditate in His temple.
For in the day of trouble He will conceal me
     in His tabernacle;
In the secret place of His tent he will hide me;
He will lift me up on a rock.
And now my head will be lifted up above my
     enemies around me,
And I will offer in His tent sacrifices
     with shouts of joy;
I will sing, yes, I will sing praises to the LORD.

Hear, O LORD, when I cry with my voice,
And be gracious to me and answer me.
When You said, "Seek My face,"
     my heart said to You,
"Your face, O LORD, I shall seek."
Do not hide Your face from me,
Do not turn Your servant away in anger;
Thou hast been my help;
Do not abandon me nor forsake me,

O God of my salvation!
For my father and my mother have
        forsaken me,
But the LORD will take me up.

Teach me Your way, O LORD,
And lead me in a level path
Because of my foes.
Do not deliver me over to the desire of my
        adversaries,
For false witnesses have risen against me,
And such as breathe out violence.
I would have despaired unless I had believed
        that I would see the goodness of the LORD
In the land of the living.
Wait for the LORD;
Be strong, and let your heart take courage;
    Yes, wait for the LORD.

Timeless Truths:

_____
_____
_____
_____
_____

Personal Application:

_____
_____
_____
_____
_____

Memory Verse

Tuck Psalm 14:2 into the creases of your mind. The verse reminds you that seeking God is a wise endeavor. Also, ask the Lord to help you to deepen relationships you have with non-Christians. Look for opportunities, or teachable moments, when it would be appropriate to share Christ with them, using the one-verse method in John 3:16.

CHAPTER SEVEN

The truth of the matter is, we all come to prayer with a tangled mass of motives— altruistic and selfish, merciful and hateful, loving and bitter. Frankly, this side of eternity we will never unravel the good from the bad, the pure from the impure. But what I have come to see is that God is big enough to receive us with all our mixture. We do not have to be bright, or pure, or filled with faith, or anything. That is what grace means, and not only are we saved by grace, we live by it as well. And we pray by it.[1]

—Richard J. Foster

Seeking God through Prayer

One day his five-year-old sauntered into Dwight L. Moody's study. The renowned evangelist was writing. Somewhat irritated by the unexpected interruption, Moody gruffly asked, "Well, what do you want?"

"Nothing, Daddy," his son replied. "I just wanted to be where you are!"

Later, a somber Moody said his son taught him a valuable lesson on the ultimate purpose of prayer:

not to ask God for a favor, but just to enjoy His companionship.[2]

Wanting to be where God is. Isn't that what prayer is all about? Don't view prayer as a "last resort." As a spiritual obligation. As a burdensome regulation. No doubt there's discipline involved. Conversing with the Lord isn't always something we feel like doing. Yet view it as a means of expressing love to God and becoming more intimate with Him.

Graze on what several spiritual giants said about prayer:

> The greatest thing anyone can do for God and for man is pray. It is not the only thing. But it is the chief thing. The great people of the earth today are the people who pray. I do not mean those who talk about prayer; nor those who say they believe in prayer; nor yet those who can explain about prayer; but I mean these people who take time and pray. THEY HAVE NOT TIME. IT MUST BE TAKEN FROM SOMETHING ELSE. This something else is important. Very important and pressing, but still less important and less pressing than prayer.   —S.D. Gordan

> The moment you wake up each morning, all your wishes and hopes for the day rush at you like wild animals. And the first job each morning consists in shoving it all back; in listening to that other voice, taking that other point of view, letting that other, larger, stronger, quieter life come flowing in.   —C.S. Lewis

If I should neglect to pray but a single day, I should lose a great deal of the fire of faith.
—Martin Luther

What the church needs today is not more or better machinery, not new organizations or more novel methods, but men whom the Holy Ghost can use. Men of prayer, men mighty in prayer.
—E.M. Bounds

God never denied that soul anything that went as far as heaven to ask for it.
—John Trapp

You can do more than pray, after you have prayed, but you cannot do more than pray until you have prayed.
—John Bunyan

Prayer will make a man cease from sin, or sin will entice a man to cease from prayer.
—John Bunyan

Q Which quotation about prayer impressed you most? Why?

A _____

_____

_____

_____

You've learned that knowing God requires a conscious choice to seek Him. You seek Him correctly when you read His Word (Chapter 6), as well as when you communicate with Him through prayer.

Benefits of Praying

What motivated men like Luther, Lewis and Bunyan to say those things about prayer? They experienced its benefits! They knew firsthand the value of communicating consistently with God. **Look up the verses that follow and pinpoint a few of the benefits they experienced.**

Q 1. John 16:24

A _____

_____

_____

_____

Q 2. Matthew 7:7-8

A _____

_____

_____

_____

Q 3. Philippians 4:6-7

A _____

_____

_____

_____

Q 4. James 1:5

A _____
_____
_____
_____

Q 5. Luke 22:31-32

A _____
_____
_____
_____

Overcoming Difficulties

Why is prayer so hard to do if it is so important? There are many barriers erected against prayer. They fall into three main categories: spiritual difficulties, psychological difficulties and physical difficulties.

Spiritual Difficulties

Disobedience. The first spiritual difficulty is sin. Isaiah 59:1-2 says, "Behold, the LORD's hand is not so short that it cannot save, nor is His ear so dull that it cannot hear. But your iniquities have made a separation between you and your God, and your sins have hidden His face from you so that He does not hear." Psalm 66:18 says, "If I regard wickedness in my heart, the Lord will not hear." Proverbs 28:9

says, "He who turns away his ear from listening to the law, even his prayer is an abomination."

Doubt and unbelief. James 1:6-7 says, "But he must ask in faith without any doubting, for the one who doubts is like the surf of the sea, driven and tossed by the wind. For that man ought not to expect that he will receive anything the Lord." Mark 11:24 says, "Therefore I say to you, all things for which you pray and ask, believe that you have received them, and they will be granted you." Doubt is kind of like saying, "Well, God, there's no way You can do this."

Impure motives. According to James 4:3, "You ask and do not receive, because you ask with wrong motives, so that you may spend it on your pleasures." Why are you asking for something? Is it to glorify God or to glorify yourself? God doesn't share His glory with anybody. It is His and His alone.

Marital discord. First Peter 3:7 says, "You husbands in the same way, live with your wives in an understanding way, as with someone weaker, since she is a woman; and show her honor as a fellow heir of the grace of life, so that your prayers will not be hindered." If things aren't right in your marriage, your prayer life won't be right, either.

Q When have you struggled with any of the above spiritual difficulties?

A _____

_____

_____

_____

Psychological Difficulties

Prayer is boring. Many people think prayer is boring. That's a psychological barrier. To be honest, initially prayer to you might seem boring. Yet when you begin to realize that God really does answer prayer, and that you are talking to the lover of your soul, then prayer is no longer boring. It becomes very exciting.

If you find prayer and time alone with God boring, change your routine. Introduce variety. Stop sitting there at your desk and just praying. Go for a walk, go out in your backyard under the trees and pray there. Anything to put variety back into your time alone with God.

"I don't have anything to say." One way to have something to say is to pray Scripture back to God. One morning I (Bill) prayed Philippians 1:2-5 for one of our staff. Then I prayed Philippians 1:9-11 for me. In this way: "I pray that my love would abound still more and more in real knowledge and all discernment, so that I may approve the things that are excellent, so I may be sincere and blameless until the day of Christ."

"I can't concentrate." Here are two strategies for improving concentration: write down your prayers and/or pray out loud.

"God doesn't listen to me." That isn't true. As a matter of fact, God doesn't have anything better to do than to listen to you pray. Ever thought of that? He's got the universe under control. No problem. He just spoke and it was created. He's

up in heaven waiting to listen to you because He loves you. He's your heavenly Father. Realize that He wants to talk to you and listen to you.

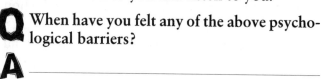 **When have you felt any of the above psychological barriers?**

_____

_____

_____

Physical Barriers

No time. If anything is important to you in life you set a time for it. You know when you're going to eat each day, you know when you're going to go to work, you know when you're going to go home. But do you know when you are going to pray? Set a time. You can pray other times, but have one set time just to pray each day. Many have found mornings to be best, but you may find it's best for you at night. It doesn't matter when. It's simply a matter of having that consistent time alone with God.

No place. Find a quiet place free of distractions.

No energy. Go to bed a few minutes earlier. If lack of energy persists, get a physical checkup.

No plan. This is a common problem. Keep on reading in this chapter and you should find some help.

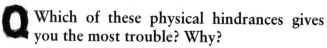 **Which of these physical hindrances gives you the most trouble? Why?**

A

Helps for Your Praying

Like personal Bible study, your prayer life blossoms when there's a structure to your time or a simple procedure to follow. Employ a five-step approach to your praying, captured in the acrostic **TALKS**. Just as a Christian seeking to know God more intimately **READS** the Bible, he also **TALKS** to God on a regular basis. The five steps that follow provide an organizational framework for your prayer times.

T = THANK GOD FOR WHAT HE HAS DONE

This aspect of prayer involves *expressing gratitude for God's deeds*. The Lord lamented the fact that the Israelites took Him for granted and "forgot His deeds" (Psalm 78:11). According to Psalm 106:7, "they did not remember" the Lord's "abundant kindnesses."

Think of some things the Lord has done for you. Include major items such as your salvation, provision of a loving spouse or the financial gift that enabled you to purchase a house. Add to your mental notes comparatively minor, yet still significant works, such as sustaining you physically after a poor night's sleep or transforming your attitude about a new project your boss assigned. Now pluck one item off your mental notepad and record it below. This should be a divine deed that you often take for granted or a recent example of His faithfulness for which you have failed to express your thanks.

 Don't proceed to the next paragraph until you pause and thank Him.

A = ADORE GOD FOR WHO HE IS

Whereas thanksgiving stems from God's provision, adoration is a *response to God Himself.* Now your attention shifts from God's deeds to His attributes. Scripture teems with lists of His character traits. The psalmist exhorts us to "Enter . . . His courts with praise" because "the LORD is good; His lovingkindness is everlasting and His faithfulness to all generations" (Psalm 100:4-5). Adjectives that describe Him include creative, wise, holy, unchanging, powerful, jealous, just, forgiving and all-knowing. Adoring Him is worshiping Him for one or more traits mentioned in Scripture or illustrated in His deeds.

Q **Which attribute of God means most to you right now? Why?**

A _____

_____

_____

_____

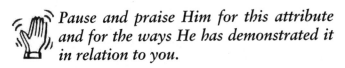 *Pause and praise Him for this attribute and for the ways He has demonstrated it in relation to you.*

L = LISTEN FOR GOD'S GUIDANCE

Contrary to many folks' perception, prayer is not a one-sided conversation. As you communicate with the Lord, He may speak to you or prompt your heart in some particular way. David exhibited a listening posture when he wrote, "Let me hear Your lovingkindness in the morning; for I trust in You; teach me the way in which I should walk" (143:8).

God won't speak audibly to you, yet in a sense His voice is louder than that. It's an inward impression given by the Holy Spirit who resides in you. What you "hear" may be the Lord pointing out an unconfessed sin, reminding you of someone who needs your encouragement or prayers, or clarifying a biblical principle that helps you make a decision. Normally, your experience of "listening to God" and "hearing Him speak" is linked to the Scriptures you read prior to your prayer time. Since His written Word is His primary means of communicating with you, inner promptings of the Holy Spirit stem from, or correlate with, what He says in the Bible. He will never tell you anything subjectively during a time of prayer that contradicts something He has already said objectively in His Word.

Listening requires a few moments of unhurried contemplation. Consult Psalm 27 again—the passage in which you practiced the **READS** Bible study method. After reading it over, be still for a moment and record here any impressions you sense God is placing on your heart.

Q Using the psalm as fuel for your thinking and praying, what is the Holy Spirit saying to you?

A _____

_____

_____

_____

_____

K = KEEP YOUR SINS CONFESSED

That means to stay up-to-date in confessing sins. A prerequisite to spiritual health is not letting much time elapse between your awareness of wrongdoing and confessing it to the Lord. If we approach Him with any other form of prayer, unconfessed sin blocks communication. "If I regard wickedness in my heart, the LORD will not hear" (Psalm 66:18).

Yet He responds favorably to honest admission of our failures. "I acknowledged my sin to You, and my iniquity I did not hide; I said, 'I will confess my transgressions to the LORD'; and You forgave the guilt of my sin" (32:5).

Often you are aware of a sin the instant it occurs, such as when you make conscious choices to disregard a biblical command or principle. But other shortcomings aren't exposed until you pause for a time of Bible reading and prayer. As you talk with God, give the Holy Spirit permission to point out decisions, bits of conversations or attitudes that displeased Him. "Listen" to His commentary on your last twenty-four hours and acknowledge the deficiencies He points out.

Right now, ponder the decisions, events and relationships that filled your last twenty-four hours. Ask the Lord to expose any behaviors or attitudes that fell short of His standards. Summarize below what He shows you:

_____

_____

_____

_____

_____

 Engage in a time of confession to Him as you deem necessary.

S = SEEK GOD'S PROVISION FOR YOURSELF AND OTHERS

Since prayer is communication with your loving heavenly Father, *say whatever is on your heart.* Tell Him your fears, your doubts, your dreams—you name it! Don't hesitate to mention your needs and make requests. Don't perceive "asking" as an immature form of prayer. Richard Foster explains why petitionary prayer is so integral to maintaining a close relationship with the Lord.

> Some have suggested that while the less discerning will continue to appeal to God for aid, the real masters of the spiritual life go beyond petition to adoring God's essence with no needs or requests whatever. In this view, our asking represents a more crude and naive form of prayer. . . . This, I submit to you, is a false spirituality. Petitionary prayer remains primary throughout our lives because we are forever dependent upon God. It is something that we never really "get beyond."[3]

Whether you make requests for yourself or for someone else, write them in a notebook, along with the date of entry. Also record when and how God answers. In the future, consulting a personal history of petitions and God's responses will provide a boost to your faith.

Q What is on your heart right now that you want to say to God?

A

Share your feelings and requests with Him at this time.

Memorizing Scripture

Your memory verse for this chapter is Psalm 63:1. Tuck the words into your heart.

The truth that Christ wants my fellowship, that He loves me, wants me to be with Him, wants to be with me and waits for me, has done more to transform my quiet time with God than any other single fact.[1]

—Robert Munger

Seeking God through Time Alone with Him

Imagine that a young man and woman are in love with each other. They spend an entire day together, yet they are in the company of other people, part of a group outing. Will cultivating their relationship exclusively in such a setting satisfy them?

Not likely! They would consider the day incomplete if they didn't reserve at least a few minutes to be alone, away from the crowd. They yearn for a special time of undistracted, heart-to-heart communication. No matter how much they enjoy each other's presence in the routine of the day, nothing solidifies their relationship like giving each other focused attention.

There's a parallel between the couple's love relationship and your companionship with the Lord.

No matter how much you try to involve Him in the routines of work, relationships and family responsibilities, you also need undistracted times when you give Him focused attention.

Back in Chapter 3, you learned that loving God is a lifestyle that involves cultivating a consciousness of Him no matter where you are or what you do throughout the day. You saw the example of Brother Lawrence, who enjoyed moment-by-moment fellowship with God as he engaged in daily routines. He modeled what is called "practicing the presence of God" in the midst of other activities. Then you received practical tips for "practicing the Lord's presence" as you proceeded through the day.

As you yourself have tried to practice the presence of God, you may have found it difficult to concentrate on the Lord while engaging in the duties of family and work. The press of responsibilities and people in your sphere of influence distract you. Brother Lawrence would be the first to admit that moment-by-moment fellowship throughout the day is a lot harder to achieve in modern society than in the era in which he lived. Traffic jams, kids' sports activities, television and shopping malls didn't compete for his attention.

The difficulty of practicing God's presence throughout the day elevates the significance of a set time to be alone with Him. Getting to know Him better and deepening your love for Him necessarily requires you to designate a time each day during which you give Him your undivided attention. This meeting with God is called a *"quiet time"* because you remove the noise and distractions that normally vie for your attention.

The last two chapters covered two basic ways to seek God: Bible reading and prayer. You practiced a **READS** approach to understanding Scripture, and a **TALKS** method to enhance your prayers. Bible reading and prayer are the two primary components of time alone with God. The diagram above shows how the previous chapters connect with this chapter. Try to fill in the blanks without referring to previous pages in this discipleship book. Write the key word starting with each letter. (For example: R= READ.)

HEART-TO-HEART COMMUNICATION
IN TIME ALONE WITH GOD

BIBLE	PRAYER
R _____	T _____
E _____	A _____
A _____	L _____
D _____	K _____
S _____	S _____

MAXIMIZING YOUR TIME
ALONE WITH GOD

In this chapter, you'll learn that establishing a daily quiet time is a choice you must make. It is not something you will always feel like doing. And you'll add to Chapters 6 and 7 by receiving more practical pointers that maximize your time alone with God.

Gaining Perspective

Cultivating the habit of a daily quiet time requires gaining an overarching perspective about Christian living. To what extent is spiritual growth a work of God? To what extent are *we* responsible for our progress in the faith? Addressing those questions involves a look at the role of your choices in spiritual development.

One hindrance to making personal devotions a habit is a misunderstanding about *how* we acquire holiness and deepen our walk with God. There are two extreme viewpoints concerning the process of spiritual nurture. Here's one author's description of these contrasting opinions and their negative effects.

> One extreme position is that spiritual growth has been left entirely up to us. By the exercise of sheer human willpower and determination alone, we attain greater and greater righteousness and live more effectively as Christians. In other words, the Lord has saved us, and now the ball is in our court. This view excessively elevates, or warps, the role of self-discipline. People who go

this route tend to give up after a while. Repeated failure causes frustration, and they wonder why they can't measure up. Though it contains a measure of truth, this approach to Christian growth is unbalanced and unbiblical. It doesn't take seriously the limitations (caused by the sin nature) of our mere human willpower and self-effort. It forgets that even after we're saved, *inner transformation is still the work of God.* Just as we cannot receive salvation apart from His grace, we cannot take steps of Christian growth without His initiative and direct involvement in our lives.

On the other hand, some Christians swing the pendulum too far in the opposite direction. They acknowledge the insufficiency of human strivings and conclude: "Since righteousness is always a result of God's grace, let's simply have faith and wait for Him to work in our lives. There is nothing we can do to facilitate the process."

This extreme position sounds spiritual enough, but it is also imbalanced and unbiblical. People with this mind-set de-emphasize the role of discipline. Some even shun spiritual discipline for fear of becoming legalistic. This attitude misinterprets "live by faith" (Galatians 2:20) to mean that God requires no human effort to live a holy life. It elevates God's provision for daily living at the expense of our clear-cut responsibility to obey Him.[2]

If neither extreme adequately explains the role of discipline, then the truth is somewhere in the middle. *Spiritual growth is both a divine work and a human re-*

sponsibility. God changes and accomplishes the growth, and He does so through "means of grace" such as Bible study and prayer. Yet engaging in Bible study and prayer involves a conscious choice on our part to spend undistracted time with Him.

Put simply, spiritual growth is a divine work because it is the Spirit of God who transforms us. Yet God has chosen to work in our hearts in response to our choice to spend time in Bible reading and prayer. So human responsibility is also involved. A person must choose to use the means of growth God has made available. When you choose to read the Bible and pray, you are placing yourself before God so He can work in you. That's how you tap into His life-changing power.

Let's review.

Q 1. **In your own words, describe the viewpoint that overemphasizes your part in spiritual growth.**

A _____

_____

_____

_____

Q 2. **Summarize the position that de-emphasizes your responsibility.**

A _____

_____

_____

_____

Q 3. Robertson McQuilkin said, "It is easier to go to a consistent extreme than to stay at the center of biblical tension."[3] **Why do you agree or disagree with this statement?**

A _____

_____

_____

Q 4. **Choice plays a part in your walk with God because . . .**

A _____

_____

_____

_____

Deciding Your Priorities

The word "priority" means *something that takes precedence in time, or superiority in rank or position.* Our responsibility is to make time alone with God a top-shelf priority. We give Him precedence when we soak up what He tells us in His Word, and when we communicate with Him. What indicates that He has a superior rank in our lives isn't what we say about Him, but making room for Him in our schedules.

Moses presented himself to God *in the morning.* "So be ready *by morning,* and come up *in the morning* to Mount Sinai, and present yourself there to Me on the top of the mountain" (Exodus 34:2, emphasis added). So did David: *"In the morning*, O LORD, You will hear my voice; *in the morning* I will order my prayer to You" (Psalm 5:3, emphasis added). Jesus apparently followed the same pattern. "*In the early morning*, while it was still dark, Jesus got up, left the house, and went away to a secluded place, and was praying there" (Mark 1:35, emphasis added). Daniel knelt for prayer "*three times a day*, praying and giving thanks before his God" (Daniel 6:10, emphasis added).

Though morning is the time most often mentioned in Scripture for a quiet time with God, no particular time slot is commanded. What matters is spending time alone with Him, not where you write His name on the page of your calendar.

Q What time of day is best for you to reserve for heart-to-heart interaction with the Lord?

A _____

_____

_____

Q What obstacles are you likely to face as you strive to keep this daily appointment with Him?

A _____

_____

_____

Selecting a Place

To build consistency, select a regular place for your appointment with the Lord. Find a particular spot that you can associate with your quiet time. The recliner by the fireplace? The desk in your home office? The kitchen table? What matters with the location is your own comfort and the absence of distractions. You can pray behind the wheel of your van, except it is difficult to have a "quiet time" while horns blare during an interstate traffic jam! So choose a time and place free from distractions, where the Lord receives your undivided attention.

Q What location will enable you to seek the Lord without the likelihood of interruptions?

A _____

_____

_____

_____

Determining a Plan

Develop a simple strategy or format for your quiet time. Though there is no hard and fast rule, here's a plan or sequence many believers follow.
1. Start with your Bible reading, employing the **READS** method explained in Chapter 6.
2. Employ the **TALKS** procedure for a time of concentrated prayer. There's a logical reason for scheduling your prayer time after your Bible reading. What you read may evoke praise, motivate intercession or reveal a need for confession. You can add these Scripture-spawned prayers to other items on your list.

3. Set a realistic time frame for your devotions. It's better to shoot for ten minutes when you are just starting out rather than thirty minutes or longer. If necessary, spread the steps in the **READS** and **TALKS** method out over several days. Just be sure to incorporate some aspects of both reading and prayer into each appointment with the Lord.

   A realistic amount of time for me to spend alone with God each day is _____.

4. Employ a pen and notebook during your quiet time. To your Bible reading notes, add specific prayer requests. Writing your requests, then recording how God answered, will produce a journal that will serve as a faith-booster for you in the future. (See the Daily Prayer Journal in Appendix B, pages 175-176.)

5. To prevent your mind from wandering, try praying aloud or varying your physical posture as you pray.

Memorizing Scripture

Go over Psalm 27:4 until you can recite it perfectly.

Don't give up on practicing the presence of God throughout the day. Merely add a daily quiet time so you can give God your undistracted attention for at least a few minutes. When your group meets again, come prepared to report on how spending time alone with God goes this week.

Scripture . . . knows nothing of solitary religion. The salvation it witnesses to is emphatically one which has corporate dimensions. No person can be reconciled to God without being reconciled to the people of God within whom his experience of God's grace immediately sets him.[1]

—Bruce Milne

Seeking God through Other Christians

Once when I (Terry) experienced a deep personal crisis, I received loving support from two Christian friends. They visited my home, treated me to breakfast and wrote notes of encouragement to sustain me over a period of several weeks. I wrote the following poem to my companions as a way of expressing gratitude.

The load is heavy. My body is bent.
My spirit too is weak and spent.
Darkness hovers, though the sun is high.
I'm too tired to pray; too numb to cry.
Feeling hopeless . . . on a downward slide.
Then you knock, and come alongside.

> Encouraging words, a listening ear. . .
> I'm reassured that Christ is near.
>
> When pain turns the heart to stone,
> No one should have to go it alone.
> In time and space, through thick and thin,
> God wraps His love in human skin.

The support I received and my reciprocation by means of a poem illustrate the significance of fellowship in the life of a Christian. Though coming to Christ involves an individual decision that no one else can make for us, spiritual growth occurs in a corporate context called "the church." God never meant for anyone in His family to go it alone.

As we have discovered in previous chapters, God meets and empowers us when we choose to seek Him. Seeking Him correctly requires cultivating the habits of talking to God through prayer and reading His Word, the Bible. But the picture would be incomplete if space was not reserved for the theme of fellowship. Seeking the Lord isn't exclusively a private matter. One factor that enhances our growth and draws us even closer to God is qualitative relationships with other believers.

This chapter tackles the question, "How does genuine fellowship show?" By examining key relational commands given to New Testament churches, we get a peek at how God defines fellowship and the type of horizontal relationships that enhance our spiritual development. The quality of your fellowship with other Christians will determine the extent to which we know and love God, thus the extent to which our lives glorify Him.

Expressions of Fellowship

After you read each Scripture reference, jot down in your own words at least one way in which fellowship shows. Each set of verses discloses at least one relational command that applies to Christians of all eras and in all geographical locations.

Q 1. Galatians 6:2

A _____

_____

_____

Q 2. Ephesians 4:32

A _____

_____

Q 3. Colossians 3:16

A _____

_____

_____

Q 4. Hebrews 10:24-25

A _____

_____

_____

Q 5. First Peter 4:10

A _____
_____
_____

Q 6. Second Corinthians 1:3-6

A _____
_____
_____

Q 7. Ephesians 4:2

A _____
_____
_____

Q 8. Ephesians 6:18-19

A _____
_____
_____

Q 9. Romans 12:10

A _____
_____
_____

Q 10. Romans 12:13

A _____

Q 11. Romans 12:17-21

A _____

Q 12. Romans 15:7

A _____

Now that you've identified relational commands that should mark interaction among Christians, mull over the following commentary. The word studies and explanations will enhance your understanding of God's relational expectations.

- **Galatians 6:2.** Bearing each other's burdens requires that we be transparent people, who let others know when we need their prayers and support. The word "burden" was used of an overloaded cargo ship in Paul's day. The load was more than the ship was intended to bear.

Similarly, when we're overloaded, we
need others to relieve us of the burden.

- **Ephesians 4:32.** Our basis for being able to
forgive someone is the phrase "as Christ
also has forgiven you." We can extend forgiveness to others because we have received
the Lord's forgiveness. And no one has hurt
us as much as our sins have hurt God.
When we picture the face of a person who
has hurt us, we can "cross out" that face—
imagine the cross of Jesus Christ superim-
posed over their facial image. That will remind us of how much we've been forgiven,
and facilitate our forgiveness of others.

- **Colossians 3:16.** What qualifies us to
"[teach] and [admonish] one another"?
The prerequisite is the phrase, "Let the
Word of Christ richly dwell within you."
A working knowledge of God's Word enables us to share with others in our sphere
of influence. To "admonish" means "to
warn." We admonish a brother or sister
in Christ when we gently warn them of
the painful consequences of inappropri-
ate behavior.

- **Hebrews 10:24-25.** The verb "to encourage" in Scripture literally means "to come
alongside." Jesus employed the noun form
of this word to describe the Holy Spirit.
He's the "Paraclete," "Comforter" or

"Helper" who figuratively comes alongside in our time of need (John 14:16).

- **First Peter 4:10.** Exercising our spiritual gifts is an expression of fellowship. The fact that no believer has all the gifts demonstrates the concept of *interdependence*. No matter what spiritual gifts we have, we still need the ministries of other believers to make us spiritually whole.

- **Second Corinthians 1:3-6.** What enabled Paul to exercise a ministry of comfort toward Christians in Corinth was his own experience of trials, combined with his experience of God's comfort during those rough times. People whom God has sustained during painful experiences make the best comforters.

- **Ephesians 4:2.** To show "tolerance" to one another means "to endure with patience." We need to give each other some "slack" since none of us is perfect.

- **Ephesians 6:18-19.** A concrete expression of fellowship is interceding for each other before the Lord. When we seek God's intervention on behalf of another, we are "rebelling against the status quo in their lives." (Other passages that focus on the ministry of intercession include Nehemiah 1:1-11, and Colossians 4:12-13. John 17 includes Jesus' prayer on behalf of His disciples.)

- **Romans 12:10.** Devotion to one another shows when we "give preference" to one another. The phrase means "to outdo one another in showing honor" or "to take the lead in making others look good." A prime example is a pianist who accompanies a soloist. The purpose of the pianist is to put the spotlight on the singer, not draw attention to his own skill. A good accompanist can actually make adjustments that cover up minor mistakes by the soloist. The accompanist takes the initiative to draw attention to the singer, not to the piano.

- **Romans 12:13.** Meeting material and emotional needs is integral to fellowship. The term "hospitality" in the New Testament carries the concept of *shelter* as well as *healing.* To practice the ministry of hospitality requires a "God's property" mind-set toward our resources. The Philippians gave sacrificially to Paul's ministry (Philippians 4:15-19). Paul implied that meeting each other's material needs creates a bond between the givers and the recipients (2 Corinthians 9:12-15).

- **Romans 12:17-21.** Even when church members sin against us, *we're responsible for how we respond!* We don't have to seek revenge because God will eventually deal with everyone who sins against us. By treating others better than they deserve, "You

will heap burning coals on his head."
Here's an explanation of that analogy:

In ancient days, homes were heated and meals
were fixed on a small portable stove, somewhat like
our outside barbecue grills. Frequently, a person
would run low on hot coals and would need to re-
plenish his supply. The container was commonly
carried on the head. So as the individual passed beneath second-story windows, thoughtful people
who had extra hot coals in their possession would
reach out of the window and place them in the
container atop his head. Thanks to the thoughtful
generosity of a few folks, he would arrive at the site
with a pile of burning coals on his head and a
ready-made fire for cooking and keeping warm.
"Heaping burning coals on someone's head" came
to be a popular expression for a spontaneous and
courteous act one person would voluntarily do for
another.[2]

- **Romans 15:7.** The Greek term translated
  "accept" means to welcome someone into
  your own inner circle of friends. The concept is one of unconditional love and implies a conscious choice to treat someone
  warmly as a member of God's family.

Experiences of Fellowship

Q 1. Look over the various expressions of fellowship once again. **Describe past experiences when you were on the receiving end of
one of these relational commands.**

A Episode #1 _____

_____

_____

A Episode #2 _____

_____

_____

Q 2. How did those experiences of Christian fellowship affect your relationship with the Lord?

A _____

_____

_____

Q 3. Which expression of fellowship from the
Bible search do you most need to experience
in your life right now? Why?

A _____

_____

Q 4. Ask the Lord to reveal the name of an individual or family in your church who needs
to receive one of these expressions of fellowship. Think of persons who are sick, unem-
ployed, alone or in need of forgiveness or
prayer. Put the name of the person or family
here:_____.

Think of this person's (or family's) need, as well
as your particular gifts and resources. **Specifically,**

how can you demonstrate the distinctiveness of authentic fellowship this week?

A _____

_____

_____

_____

Memorizing Scripture

Add Psalm 119:2 to your memory bank.

A clear conscience is an inner freedom of spirit which comes from knowing that no one is able to point a finger at me and accuse me of wrongs I have not made right.[1]

—Joe Aldrich

CHAPTER
TEN

Seeking God with a Clean Heart

A conscience-stricken taxpayer sent the following letter to the Internal Revenue Service:

Dear Sir:

My conscience bothered me. Here is the $125 I owe in back taxes.

There was a P.S. at the bottom, which read:

If my conscience still bothers me, I'll send the rest.[2]

The taxpayer's response is humorous and, from an ethical standpoint, incomplete. Yet it reveals the importance of our conscience in maintaining personal purity and a right relationship with the Lord.

So far in this course you have identified the ultimate purpose of Christian living: to glorify God. He is honored when you love Him. Loving Him depends on, and is intensified by, knowing Him ever more intimately. When you get to know Him personally by receiving Christ as your Savior, you naturally want others to know Him too. Then for the rest of your life, grow closer to Him by choosing to seek Him through avenues He Himself has established: by reading His Word, praying, establishing a daily quiet time and experiencing authentic fellowship with other Christians.

Yet seeking God with the right habits is not enough to insure a close relationship. A right heart must accompany our efforts to build a relationship with Him. That point brings you to this current chapter. One characteristic of a right heart is purity. Keeping your heart right before God requires a sensitivity to sin that the Holy Spirit exposes in your life and regular times of confession that result in a clear conscience.

Definition of "Conscience"

What is the "conscience"? In Acts 24:16 Paul gives a clue. He wrote, "I also do my best to maintain always a blameless conscience both before God and before men." A clear conscience means we are blameless in thought, word and deed in our relationship with God as well as with other people. Blameless doesn't suggest perfection. But it implies that when we become aware of a sin or offense, we admit it and ask to be forgiven. Put simply, we keep "short accounts" with God and other people.

Here's how Joe Aldrich clarified the meaning of "conscience" in a believer's life:

> [A conscience is a] red warning light on our spiritual dashboard which tells us that something is wrong in the heart . . . or a spiritual magnetic north pole which assures us that we are navigating within the boundary conditions of God's character.
>
> A clear conscience is an inner freedom of spirit which comes from knowing that no one is able to point a finger at me and accuse me of wrongs I have not made right.[3]

Consequences of a Guilty Conscience

When we allow unconfessed sin to mar our conscience, our relationship with the Lord suffers.

Q **What consequences do the following verses mention?**

A • Psalm 66:18 _____

_____

_____

_____

A • Psalm 32:3-4 _____

_____

_____

_____

A • First Timothy 1:18-19 _____

_____

_____

_____

Joe Aldrich puts a cap on the issue of consequences:

> There is a direct correlation between the
> condition of my conscience and my ability to
> witness, my effectiveness in resisting tempta-
> tion, my ability to make wise decisions, and my
> capacity to develop significant friendships.[4]

Q Think about times in your past when you vio-
lated your conscience in some manner. **What
damaging consequences did you experience?**

A _____
_____
_____
_____
_____

Q Specifically, how did a guilty conscience affect your relationship with the Lord?

A _____
_____
_____
_____

Steps to a Clear Conscience

Acquiring and maintaining a clear conscience requires self-examination in light of biblical standards. Many people have found it helpful to read
Jesus' "Sermon on the Mount" in Matthew 5-7.
The theme of this passage is "Christians are differ-

ent." Jesus explains character qualities and behavior that should distinguish a Christian from a non-Christian.

On the pages that follow, read each excerpt from Jesus' sermon, as well as the verses that provide a context from Matthew 5-7. Then answer each of the corresponding questions. Reserve a time when you will have thirty to forty-five uninterrupted minutes, for this is an extensive, reflective exercise. (You may want to do this during your time alone with God.) Ask the Lord to convict you of impurities or behaviors that are staining your heart. If you're a sensitive, serious Christian, you may have a tendency to be too hard on your self. Reply honestly, yet try to distinguish between your own perfection or tendency toward self-condemnation and the conviction of the Holy Spirit. As you begin, make Psalm 139:23-24 your prayer: "Search me, O God, and know my heart; try me and know my anxious thoughts; and see if there be any hurtful way in me, and lead me in the everlasting way."

1. Blessed are the poor in spirit. (See Matthew 5:3.)

   • Are you proud?

   • Do you draw attention to yourself or your accomplishments?

   • Do you put your desires above Christ's?

2. Blessed are those who mourn. (See Matthew 5:4.)

   • Do you have a lack of concern for people's needs?

- Does the presence of sin in your life cause you to grieve?

- Do you take the lost condition of your unsaved friends too casually?

3. Blessed are the gentle. (See Matthew 5:5.)

    - Have you been insensitive to the emotional needs of others?

    - Are you abrasive and uncaring?

    - Do you intentionally hurt people's feelings?

4. Blessed are those who hunger and thirst for righteousness. (See Matthew 5:6.)

    - Is happiness more important to you than holiness?

    - Do you yearn to be godly?

    - Are you unconcerned about walking in righteousness?

5. Blessed are the merciful. (See Matthew 5:7.)

    - Is there anyone you know to whom you have not shown mercy?

    - Do you ever secretly rejoice when someone else suffers?

    - Have you failed to show more mercy to those less fortunate?

6. Blessed are the pure in heart. (See Matthew 5:8.)

    - Are you driven by impure motives?

    - Do you tend to manipulate others?

- Have you wanted to gain recognition from others?

7. Blessed are the peacemakers. (See Matthew 5:9.)

- Do you fuss and fight with family or friends?
- Do you always try to have the last word?
- Are you reluctant to say, "I'm sorry"?

8. Blessed are those who have been persecuted for the sake of righteousness. . . . Rejoice, and be glad. (See Matthew 5:10-12.)

- Do you often feel ashamed of Christ when you are around others?
- Have you avoided standing up for Him?
- Have you complained about persecution?

9. Let your light shine before men in such a way that they may see your good works. (See Matthew 5:16.)

- Do you have friends who do not realize that you are a Christian?
- Have you tried to be one of the crowd?
- Have you failed to tell others that Christ is why you act as you do?

10. Whoever then annuls one of the least of these commandments, and teaches others to do the same, shall be called least in the kingdom of heaven. (See Matthew 5:19.)

- Have you considered any of God's Word as unimportant?

- Do you justify your actions, disregarding God's Word?

- Have you led others astray by your disobedience?

11. Everyone who is angry with his brother shall be guilty before the court. (See Matthew 5:21-26.)

    - Are you easily angered?

    - Are there people toward whom you feel anger or bitterness now? Why?

12. Everyone who looks at a woman with lust for her has already committed adultery with her in his heart. (See Matthew 5:27-32.)

    - Is lust a recurring problem for you?

    - Are you exposing yourself to people or media that tend to fuel lust?

    - Are you involved in any immoral relationship?

13. Let your statement be, "Yes, yes" or "No, no"; anything beyond these is of evil. (See Matthew 5:33-37.)

    - Is your word reliable?

    - Can you spot evidences of irresponsibility in your life?

    - Have you failed to follow through on your commitments?

14. Whoever slaps you on your right cheek, turn the other to him also. (See Matthew 5:38-42.)

    - Are you quick to get revenge?

- When others sin against you, is it your tendency to get even?
- Have you failed to give others a second chance?

15. Love your enemies and pray for those who persecute you. (See Matthew 5:43-48.)

- Do you hate anyone?
- Have you failed to pray for those who persecute you or mistreat you?
- Have you failed to do good to those who do bad to you?

16. Beware of practicing your righteousness before men to be noticed by them. (See Matthew 6:1.)

- Do you try to impress people?
- Do you have to be the center of attention?
- Do you engage in "spiritual" things just so others will notice?

17. When . . . you give to the poor. (See Matthew 6:2-4.)

- Have you failed to tithe—that is, give ten percent of your income to God?
- Do you give to God with a grudge?
- Have you failed to give sacrificially?

18. When you pray. . . . (See Matthew 6:5-13.)

- When you pray publicly, do you think about the people who are listening in?
- Are your prayers sincere?

- When you say, "I will pray for you," do you follow through?

19. If you forgive men for their transgressions, your heavenly Father will also forgive you. (See Matthew 6:14-15.)

    - Is there someone you haven't forgiven?

    - Are you holding any grudges?

    - Do you remind others of past offenses?

20. Whenever you fast. . . . (See Matthew 6:16-18.)

    - Have you failed to fast?

    - Do your appetites control you?

    - Do you let others know when you're fasting?

21. Do not store up for yourselves treasures on earth. (See Matthew 6:19-21.)

    - Are there things in your life which are more important than Christ?

    - Do you tend to idolize your possessions?

    - Have you failed to "store up . . . treasures in heaven"?

22. The eye is the lamp of the body; so then if your eye is clear, your whole body will be full of light. (See Matthew 6:22-23.)

    - Are you envious of anyone or covetous of anything?

    - Have you been exposing yourself to ungodly magazines?

- Have you been watching any sensual programs or movies?

23. Do not be worried. . . . (See Matthew 6:25-32.)

- Do you worry more than you pray about material needs?

- Do you complain often about your physical/material status?

- When you trust God for His provision, how does it show?

24. Seek first His kingdom and His righteousness. (See Matthew 6:33-34.)

- Has God slipped from first place in your life?

- Do you give God your focused attention on a daily basis?

- Have you let unconfessed sin linger in your life?

25. Do not judge so that you will not be judged. (See Matthew 7:1-6.)

- Do you tend to judge others?

- Do you look down on anybody?

- Do you reveal a "holier than thou" attitude?

26. Ask, . . . seek, . . . knock. (See Matthew 7:7-11.)

- Do you have regular time to pray?

- Do you pray more for yourself than for others?

- Have you overlooked thanking God for His answers?

27. Treat people the same way you want them to treat you. (See Matthew 7:12.)

    - Are you actively serving others?

    - What evidences of a self-centered rather than an others-centered life do you see?

    - Are you choosy about whom you serve?

28. Enter through the narrow gate. (See Matthew 7:13-14.)

    - Have you refused to do what is right when it has been hard?

    - Do you spurn opportunities to stand up for Christ?

    - Do you give in when others coax you to do things that are wrong?

29. Every tree that does not bear good fruit is cut down and thrown into the fire. (See Matthew 7:15-20.)

    - Do others see changes in your character as a result of your faith in Christ?

    - Do the following traits mark your life: love, joy, peace, patience, kindness, goodness, faithfulness, gentleness and self-control?

30. Not everyone who says to Me, "Lord, Lord," will enter the kingdom of heaven; but he who does the will of My Father who is in heaven will enter. (See Matthew 7:21-22.)

- Are there areas in your life in which you are deliberately disobeying God?

- Are you afraid to give Christ total control of your life?

- Are you the boss of your life?

31. Everyone who hears these words of Mine and does not act upon them, may be compared to a wise man who built his house on the rock. (See Matthew 7:24-29.)

    - Do you hear God's Word and fail to do it?

    - Do you act as if God's Word is unimportant?

    - Do you regularly read God's Word and expose yourself to sound Bible teaching?

 Now that you have completed the trek through Matthew 5-7, make note of questions from the list that exposed sin. Look for patterns or trends in these questions. (For instance, some questions focus on internal attitudes or sins of the heart. Other probes put the spotlight on observable behavior.)

 Right now, take a few minutes and confess those attitudes and behaviors that the Holy Spirit has exposed. Be *specific* when you confess. For example, instead of admitting, "I've been selfish," say, "I've acted selfishly in my relationship with *(name of person)*."

When you pray about areas exposed by God's Spirit, remember the Lord's promise to forgive you. According to First John 1:9, "If we confess our sins, He is faithful and righteous to forgive us our sins and to cleanse us from all unrighteousness." The result will be a fresh intimacy with the Lord, and freedom from the burden of conviction: "Therefore there is now no condemnation for those who are in Christ Jesus" (Romans 8:1).

If you are sincere in your confession, you are not guilty before Him, no matter how you may feel. If *feelings* of guilt still badger you after you confess, remember this: God's Word says you are forgiven. *And God's Word is far more reliable than your feelings!*

 How does knowing you are forgiven make you feel? *Right now, say a prayer of thanksgiving to God that expresses your appreciation. Remember that your forgiveness cost Him the death of His Son, Jesus Christ, on the cross.*

Memorizing Scripture

Camp out in Psalm 46:10 until you can recite it from memory.

Also, review the one-verse method (John 3:16) introduced in Chapter 5. Ask God for opportunities to share it with individuals in your sphere of influence. If you ever make an appointment with a nonbeliever for the purpose of sharing John 3:16, ask another Christian to intercede for you during the appointment time.

Seeking God wholeheartedly involves submission to His rule. After all, a throne only has the seating capacity of one.

CHAPTER
ELEVEN

Seeking God with a Whole Heart

Decades ago, during the civil rights movement in the southern states of America, a Christian pondered the issue of wholehearted commitment to Jesus Christ. He observed a lot of people who wanted just enough of God to guarantee escape from eternal flames, but not enough of Him to start remodeling their lifestyles. He wrote the following satirical words:

> I would like to buy $3 worth of God, please. Not enough to explode my soul or disturb my sleep, but just enough to equal a cup of warm milk or a snooze in the sunshine. I don't want enough of Him to make me love a black man or pick beets with a migrant. I want the warmth of the womb, not a new birth. I want a pound of the eternal in a paper sack. I would like to buy $3 worth of God, please.[1]

Of course, Christian discipleship isn't a commodity that we can purchase in piecemeal fashion. Following Jesus is an all-or-nothing proposition. Either

He is master of our lives or He isn't. Knowing Him better involves not only seeking Him with a *clean* heart (Chapter 10), but also seeking Him with a *whole* heart.

All-or-Nothing Commitment

Imagine a man proposes to a woman. He tells her in flowery language what a loyal, loving and committed husband he'll be to her—*364 days a year*! Then he says he's reserving one day a year solely for himself, to satisfy whatever appetites he has. He even acknowledges that other women will be on his agenda for that one day each year.

How do you think the woman would respond to the proposal?

— Let me think about it . . .

— No way!

— Let's set a date for the wedding!

Unless she's desperate, she would voice an emphatic "NO!" to his proposal. No matter how faithful the man is 364 days a year, avoiding his commitment for even one day reveals a half-hearted devotion to his bride. His attitude toward marriage is tantamount to a believer trying to purchase "$3 worth of God." No relationship can thrive under such an arrangement.

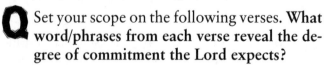 Set your scope on the following verses. **What word/phrases from each verse reveal the degree of commitment the Lord expects?**

A Deuteronomy 4:29 _____

_____

_____

A Second Chronicles 16:9 _____

_____

_____

A Jeremiah 29:13 _____

_____

_____

In a letter to a young pastor, Paul broached the issue of wholehearted devotion to the Lord. What he said to Timothy applies to every believer who strives to seek and to serve our Lord. Read Second Timothy 2:3-6 in light of the following questions.

Q What analogies, or word pictures, did Paul use to describe a devoted Christian?

A _____

_____

_____

Q What qualities was Paul promoting with the use of these analogies?

A _____

_____

_____

Q What happens when a soldier, athlete or
farmer approaches his responsibilities with a
lukewarm attitude?

A _____

_____

_____

Q In view of the points Paul made with these
three analogies, how would you describe your
current devotion to the Lord? To what extent
are you seeking Him with a whole heart?

A _____

_____

_____

Halfhearted Commitment

In Second Timothy 2:3-6, Paul suggests that a
disciple is single-minded, disciplined and diligent.
For instance, he said that no soldier who wants to
please his superior "entangles himself in the affairs
of everyday life" (2:4). Obviously, this verse does
not condemn working an eight-hour shift at the office, balancing a checkbook or attending a football
game. Yet it is a call to remove any hindrance to an

intimate relationship with God. Neither necessary duties nor leisure pursuits should keep us from seeking and obeying Him.

Seeking God with a whole heart may mean applying the following maxim: *The good is often the enemy of the best.*

What saps our energy for the Lord is not necessarily something evil or sinful. For instance, staying up late may make a morning quiet time more difficult. Working sixty hours a week may leave you no time to volunteer at your local church. Or regular weekend trips to your cabin on the lake may result in an anemic diet of Bible teaching and a deterioration of faith-strengthening fellowship. No one is advocating here a monastic existence where every waking moment is spent on spiritual disciplines or church activities. But the challenge to you is to seek God above all else; to eliminate every hindrance to cultivating a closer relationship with Him; to evaluate your stewardship of time, resources and relationships in light of their impact on your spiritual development.

Q **What are some good or wholesome things in your life that nonetheless displace time and energy that should go to God?**

A _____

_____

_____

_____

Q What concrete steps will you take to remove these hindrances to a wholehearted approach to seeking God?

A _____

_____

_____

_____

An Example of Commitment

Before the demise of communism in the former Soviet Union, it was not always easy or safe to be a Christian. The believers in the following true story sought and followed the Lord wholeheartedly, not superficially:

> An underground house church in a city of the former Soviet Union received one copy of the Gospel of Luke, the only Scripture most of these Christians had ever seen. They tore it into small sections and distributed them among the body of believers. Their plan was to memorize the portion they had been given, then on the next Lord's Day they would meet and redistribute the scriptural sections.
>
> On Sunday these believers arrived inconspicuously in small groups throughout the day so as not to arouse the suspicion of KGB informers. By dusk they were all safely inside, windows closed and doors locked. They began by singing a hymn quietly but with deep emotion. Suddenly, the door was pushed open and in walked two soldiers with loaded automatic weapons at the

ready. One shouted, "All right—everybody line up against the wall. If you wish to renounce your commitment to Jesus Christ, leave now!"

Two or three quickly left, then another. After a few more seconds, two more.

"This is your last chance. Either turn against your faith in Christ," he ordered, "or stay and suffer the consequences."

Another left. Finally, two more in embarrassed silence with their faces covered slipped out into the night. No one else moved. Parents with small children trembling beside them looked down reassuringly. They fully expected to be gunned down or, at best, to be imprisoned.

After a few moments of complete silence, the other soldier closed the door, looked back at those who stood against the wall and said, "Keep your hands up—but this time in praise to our Lord Jesus Christ, brothers and sisters. We, too, are Christians. We were sent to another house church several weeks ago to arrest a group of believers—"

The other soldier interrupted, " . . . but, instead, *we were converted!* We have learned by experience, however, that unless people are willing to die for their faith, they cannot be fully trusted."[2]

Do you yearn for their kind of wholehearted devotion to the Lord? Are you tired of mediocrity when it comes to your relationship with God?

Mull over the following remark by Isaac D'Israeli in relation to your Christian life: "It is a wretched waste to be gratified with mediocrity when the excellent lies before us."[3]

If this chapter has whetted your appetite for a wholehearted devotion to the Lord, make the following prayer your own. Sign your name in the space provided. (Warning: Don't sign the prayer casually. Praying it to God may prove hazardous to your current lifestyle.)

> *To my personal Savior, Jesus Christ. I want to be able to call You "Lord"—and mean it! I admit that other people and things in this world often compete for my allegiance to You. But You deserve my single-minded devotion. Forgive me for accepting mediocrity rather than striving for excellence in my walk with You. I give You permission to purge from my life anything that hinders me spiritually—and empower me to do my part in that removal process. From now on I am willing to die to selfish pursuits and follow You without reservation. I know that seeking You wholeheartedly will not always be easy—but it will always be right. Amen.*

Signed_____
Dated_____

Mull over Jesus' word in Luke 14:27: "Whoever does not carry his own cross and come after Me cannot be My disciple." Jesus uttered those words in the context of a talk on the cost of commitment. Back in the first century, whoever was seen "carrying his own cross" was on his way to die. Criminals who received the death penalty were executed by crucifixion. Condemned persons often lugged their own cross to the place of crucifixion. By employing this analogy, Jesus was calling for followers who are willing to die to selfish pursuits and follow Him without reservation.

Memorizing Scripture

Set your scope on Jeremiah 29:13. This verse adds an exclamation point to the issue of wholehearted devotion to God.

If only God knows what I am doing, since I know He won't tell, I tend to make all kinds of excuses for myself. But if I must report to another or a group of others, I begin to monitor my behavior. If someone is keeping an eye on me, my behavior improves.[1]

—Bruce Larsen

Looking Back . . . Going Forward

Bruce Wilkinson of Walk Thru The Bible Ministries wrote, "We wrongly believe that a greater quantity of content covered is better than a greater quantity of content learned."[2] He's an advocate of covering less material more thoroughly, instead of dumping too much content on folks all at once.

One application of his "less is more" principle is *review*. By identifying important concepts that have affected you, the truths will be tucked even deeper into the folds of your mind.

Right now, jot down responses to the following questions. Take your time and refer to previous chapters as necessary to formulate your answers.

Truth in the Rearview Mirror

Q 1. Which chapter from the *Knowing God* course had the biggest impact on you? Why?

A _____

_____

_____

_____

Q 2. What truth or insight from our Bible study encourages you most? Why?

A _____

_____

_____

_____

Q 3. Which insight that we've covered is most convicting? Why?

A _____

_____

_____

_____

Q 4. What misconceptions about Christian living have the Bible studies erased? Explain.

A _____

_____

_____

_____

Q 5. How has your relationship with the Lord changed since our group launched this course? (Please be specific.)

A _____

_____

_____

Q 6. Which Bible memory verse has affected you most? Why?

A _____

_____

_____

Q 7. What questions about getting to know God or about issues addressed in this course still linger in your mind?

A _____

_____

_____

Q 8. As a result of participating in this *Knowing God* course, what group member have you learned to appreciate most? Why?

A _____

_____

_____

Q 9. How has the presence of other believers in this study group increased your diligence in chapter application? (Be specific!)

A _____

_____

_____

_____

Practicing Accountability

Question #9 focuses on a crucial biblical concept: *accountability*. To some extent you've experienced accountability in your group meetings. You've recited memory verses to a partner. You've discussed progress in your efforts to seek God through the means of prayer, Bible reading and a daily quiet time. You devoted one chapter to the importance of fellowship, noting how "seeking God" is facilitated by applying relational commands in the New Testament.

But allow me to shine the spotlight one last time on the idea of accountability. Here's how Charles Swindoll defines the term:

> Accountability is answering the hard questions . . . opening one's life to a few carefully selected, trusted, loyal confidants who speak the truth—who have the right to examine, to question, to appraise, and to give counsel. . . . I have formed the habit of asking about accountability when stories of someone's spiritual defection or moral fall comes to my attention. Without fail, I ask something like, "Was _____ accountable to someone on a

regular basis? Did he (she) meet with one, two, or three folks for the purpose of giving and receiving counsel, prayer, and planning?" Without exception—*hear me now*—without a single exception, the answer has been the same: NO![3]

Accountability is integral to your ongoing application of this *Knowing God* course and to your ongoing passion to glorify God. The key to "keeping" this material rather than neglecting it is to maintain close ties with other believers—in one-to-one relationships, as well as through small group involvement.

Knowing God is the first of a series of basic discipleship courses from Christian Publications that your church may eventually offer. Others include *Discovering Your Identity* (experiencing security through your position in Christ), *Catching the Spirit* (Holy Spirit), *Learning to Trust* (how the Lord tests and deepens our faith) and *Sharing the Message* (how to witness effectively).

By committing to a group or class covering these other courses, you'll experience a context that will "keep you sharp" as you continue to apply *Knowing God* material. Perhaps an analogy will enhance understanding of how accountability stokes the fires of spiritual passion. Imagine you have one horse that can pull 9,000 pounds and another that can pull 8,000 pounds. Put them together, and you'd expect the team to pull no more than 17,000 pounds. But that's not the case.

Working as a team, the two horses can pull a total of 30,000 pounds! This principle is called *synergism: the simultaneous action of separate agents working together has greater total effect than the sum of their individual effort.* Inviting other believers to ask you hard questions about your walk with Christ is essential if "seeking God" is to become a habit pattern in your life.

Evaluating Your Progress

Your final group session for this course will involve a discussion of responses to questions 1-9 in this chapter. But the following checklist is **just for you,** and you won't be asked to share responses with anyone else.

Which of the following statements are true for you? Reflect on your application of truths and skills from this *Knowing God* book. Which significant steps have you taken?

• I want "glorifying and pleasing God" to be my life purpose. (Chapters 1 and 2)

Yes _____ No _____

• I am using one or more of the practical suggestions for focusing attention on God throughout the day. (Chapter 3)

Yes _____ No _____

• I have received Jesus Christ as my personal Savior, so I know Him personally instead of just knowing about Him. (Chapter 4)

Yes _____ No _____

- I've learned and shared the "one-verse" method for John 3:16 as a way to help others know Jesus Christ. (Chapter 5)

Yes _____ No _____

- I am getting to know God better by using the **READS** approach to Bible study. (Chapter 6)

Yes _____ No _____

- I am growing closer to God by using the **TALKS** approach for maximizing my prayer time. (Chapter 7)

Yes _____ No _____

- I am keeping a daily appointment with God—an undistracted time alone with Him. (Chapter 8)

Yes _____ No _____

- In order to deepen my fellowship with the Lord, I am taking steps to strengthen my fellowship with other Christians. (Chapter 9)

Yes _____ No _____

- I have examined the distinctive marks of a Christian in Matthew 5-7, and confessed patterns of disobedience as a way to purify my heart before God. (Chapter 10)

Yes _____ No _____

- I have started the process of removing hindrances to a wholehearted devotion to God. I want Jesus Christ alone to sit on the throne of my life. (Chapter 11)

Yes _____ No _____

- I have identified a way to experience accountability in my relationships with other
believers or with someone who will keep
asking me about my progress in seeking
God. (Chapter 12)

Yes _____ No _____

- I know each of the following Bible references from memory (check ones you can
still recite):

_____	Philippians 4:20	(Chapter 2)
_____	Mark 12:30	(Chapter 3)
_____	Philippians 3:8	(Chapter 4)
_____	Psalm 73:25	(Chapter 5)
_____	Psalm 14:2	(Chapter 6)
_____	Psalm 63:1	(Chapter 7)
_____	Psalm 27:4	(Chapter 8)
_____	Psalm 119:2	(Chapter 9)
_____	Psalm 46:10	(Chapter 10)
_____	Jeremiah 29:13	(Chapter 11)
_____	Second Peter 3:18	(Chapter 12)

If you did not score 100 percent, that is OK.
Change may come in small increments. The important thing is that you have started the process
of seeking God, so you can fulfill that overarching
purpose of bringing Him glory and pleasure. *Con-
gratulations on the significant steps you have
taken!* Let your recent progress serve as the impe-
tus for a lifelong journey of glorifying God by loving Him, seeking Him and serving Him. To

expedite that journey, respond to the following questions.

Q Which application from *Knowing God* are you most consistent in carrying out? Explain.

A _____

_____

_____

_____

Q Which application or significant step are you least consistent in carrying out? Explain.

A _____

_____

_____

_____

Q Now that you have completed the *Knowing God* material, what action plans do you have to develop more consistency in the deficient areas?

A _____

_____

_____

_____

Putting It All Together

Your life purpose is to glorify God. Glorifying God occurs when you fulfill the Great Commandment to love Him with all your heart,

SEEKING GOD

With the Right Habits
- Bible Study (Chapter 6)
- Prayer (Chapter 7)
- Daily Quiet Time (Chapter 8)
- Fellowship with Christians (Chapter 9)

With the Right Heart
- A Clean Heart (Chapter 10)
- A Whole Heart (Chapter 11)

RESULTS IN

KNOWING GOD and
TELLING OTHERS ABOUT HIM
(Chapter 4 and 5)

RESULTS IN
LOVING GOD
(Chapter 3)

RESULTS IN
GLORIFYING GOD
(Chapters 1 and 2)

Facing the Future with Confidence

As you face the future, be encouraged by Paul's words to believers in Philippi: "I am confident of this very thing, that He who began a good work in you will perfect it until the day of Christ Jesus" (Philippians 1:6).

Memorizing Scripture

Your final memory verse puts a clincher on the concept of glorifying God through continued spiritual growth: Second Peter 3:18.

Appendix A

Daily Bible Reading Journal

From each day's Bible reading, record one insight that God impressed upon you, as well as one specific application you identified.

Week 1

Sunday

Passage _____ Date _____

Timeless Truth: _____

_____

_____

Personal Application: _____

_____

_____

Monday

Passage _____ Date _____

Timeless Truth: _____

_____

_____

Personal Application: _____

_____

_____

TUESDAY
Passage _____   Date _____
Timeless Truth: _____
_____
_____

Personal Application: _____
_____
_____

WEDNESDAY
Passage _____   Date _____
Timeless Truth: _____
_____
_____

Personal Application: _____
_____
_____

THURSDAY
Passage _____   Date _____
Timeless Truth: _____
_____
_____

Personal Application: _____
_____
_____

FRIDAY

Passage _____   Date _____

Timeless Truth: _____

_____

_____

Personal Application: _____

_____

_____

SATURDAY

Passage _____   Date _____

Timeless Truth: _____

_____

_____

Personal Application: _____

_____

_____

WEEK 2

SUNDAY

Passage _____   Date _____

Timeless Truth: _____

_____

_____

Personal Application: _____

_____

_____

MONDAY

Passage _____   Date _____

Timeless Truth: _____

_____

_____

Personal Application: _____

_____

_____

TUESDAY

Passage _____   Date _____

Timeless Truth: _____

_____

_____

Personal Application: _____

_____

_____

WEDNESDAY

Passage _____   Date _____

Timeless Truth: _____

_____

_____

Personal Application: _____

_____

_____

THURSDAY

Passage _____   Date _____

Timeless Truth: _____

_____

_____

Personal Application: _____

_____

_____

FRIDAY

Passage _____   Date _____

Timeless Truth: _____

_____

_____

Personal Application: _____

_____

_____

SATURDAY

Passage _____   Date _____

Timeless Truth: _____

_____

_____

Personal Application: _____

_____

_____

WEEK 3

SUNDAY

Passage _____   Date _____

Timeless Truth: _____

_____

_____

Personal Application: _____

_____

_____

MONDAY

Passage _____   Date _____

Timeless Truth: _____

_____

_____

Personal Application: _____

_____

_____

TUESDAY

Passage _____   Date _____

Timeless Truth: _____

_____

_____

Personal Application: _____

_____

_____

WEDNESDAY

Passage _____   Date _____

Timeless Truth: _____

_____

_____

Personal Application: _____

_____

_____

THURSDAY

Passage _____   Date _____

Timeless Truth: _____

_____

_____

Personal Application: _____

_____

_____

FRIDAY

Passage _____   Date _____

Timeless Truth: _____

_____

_____

Personal Application: _____

_____

_____

SATURDAY

Passage _____   Date _____

Timeless Truth: _____

_____

_____

Personal Application: _____

_____

_____

WEEK 4

SUNDAY

Passage _____   Date _____

Timeless Truth: _____

_____

_____

Personal Application: _____

_____

_____

MONDAY

Passage _____   Date _____

Timeless Truth: _____

_____

_____

Personal Application: _____

_____

_____

TUESDAY

Passage _____ Date _____

Timeless Truth: _____

_____

_____

Personal Application: _____

_____

_____

WEDNESDAY

Passage _____ Date _____

Timeless Truth: _____

_____

_____

Personal Application: _____

_____

_____

THURSDAY

Passage _____ Date _____

Timeless Truth: _____

_____

_____

Personal Application: _____

_____

_____

FRIDAY
Passage _____   Date _____
Timeless Truth: _____
_____
_____

Personal Application: _____
_____
_____

SATURDAY
Passage _____   Date _____
Timeless Truth: _____
_____
_____

Personal Application: _____
_____
_____

WEEK 5
SUNDAY
Passage _____   Date _____
Timeless Truth: _____
_____
_____

Personal Application: _____
_____
_____

MONDAY

Passage _____   Date _____

Timeless Truth: _____

_____

_____

Personal Application: _____

_____

_____

TUESDAY

Passage _____   Date _____

Timeless Truth: _____

_____

_____

Personal Application: _____

_____

_____

WEDNESDAY

Passage _____   Date _____

Timeless Truth: _____

_____

_____

Personal Application: _____

_____

_____

THURSDAY

Passage _____   Date _____

Timeless Truth: _____

_____

_____

Personal Application: _____

_____

_____

FRIDAY

Passage _____   Date _____

Timeless Truth: _____

_____

_____

Personal Application: _____

_____

_____

SATURDAY

Passage _____   Date _____

Timeless Truth: _____

_____

_____

Personal Application: _____

_____

_____

WEEK 6

SUNDAY

Passage _____   Date _____

Timeless Truth: _____

_____

_____

Personal Application: _____

_____

_____

MONDAY

Passage _____   Date _____

Timeless Truth: _____

_____

_____

Personal Application: _____

_____

_____

TUESDAY

Passage _____   Date _____

Timeless Truth: _____

_____

_____

Personal Application: _____

_____

_____

WEDNESDAY

Passage _____   Date _____

Timeless Truth: _____

_____

_____

Personal Application: _____

_____

_____

THURSDAY

Passage _____   Date _____

Timeless Truth: _____

_____

_____

Personal Application: _____

_____

_____

FRIDAY

Passage _____   Date _____

Timeless Truth: _____

_____

_____

Personal Application: _____

_____

_____

SATURDAY

Passage _____   Date _____

Timeless Truth: _____

_____

_____

Personal Application: _____

_____

_____

WEEK 7

SUNDAY

Passage _____   Date _____

Timeless Truth: _____

_____

_____

Personal Application: _____

_____

_____

MONDAY

Passage _____   Date _____

Timeless Truth: _____

_____

_____

Personal Application: _____

_____

_____

TUESDAY

Passage _____   Date _____

Timeless Truth: _____

_____

_____

Personal Application: _____

_____

_____

WEDNESDAY

Passage _____   Date _____

Timeless Truth: _____

_____

_____

Personal Application: _____

_____

_____

THURSDAY

Passage _____   Date _____

Timeless Truth: _____

_____

_____

Personal Application: _____

_____

_____

FRIDAY

Passage _____   Date _____

Timeless Truth: _____

_____

_____

Personal Application: _____

_____

_____

SATURDAY

Passage _____   Date _____

Timeless Truth: _____

_____

_____

Personal Application: _____

_____

_____

APPENDIX B

DAILY PRAYER JOURNAL

The following incomplete sentences are based on the **TALKS** approach to prayer, Chapter 7 of *Knowing God*. Completing each sentence is a way to keep a compact record of your prayer times.

One thing God has done that I want to thank Him for today is

_____

_____

_____

_____

One thing about God Himself that I want to praise Him for today is

_____

_____

_____

_____

As I "listen" to God today, one thing He is trying to say to me is

_____

_____

_____

_____

A sin or shortcoming He has exposed and is nudging me to confess today is _____

_____

_____

_____

_____

A need or request I need to take before the Lord today is _____

_____

_____

_____

_____

ENDNOTES

CHAPTER 1 - Choosing a Life Purpose

1. A.W. Tozer, Man: the Dwelling Place of God (Camp Hill, PA: Christian Publications, 1997), p. 92.

2. Ibid., pp. 92-93.

3. Charles Colson, *Loving God* (Grand Rapids, MI: Zondervan, 1983), pp. 13-14.

4. Taken from a chapel message delivered by Stuart Briscoe to the student body of Wheaton College and Graduate School, April, 1972.

5. Terry Powell, *Balance Living on a Tightrope* (Wheaton, IL: Victor Books, 1990), p. 113.

CHAPTER 2 - Identifying Your Life Purpose

1. J.I. Packer, *Knowing God* (Downers Grove, IL: InterVarsity Press, 1973), p. 30.

2. Charles Swindoll, *Growing Strong in the Seasons of Life* (Portland, OR: Multnomah Press, 1983), p. 317.

3. Jim Elliot, *The Journals of Jim Elliot*, Elisabeth Elliot, ed. (Old Tappan, NJ: Fleming Revell Co., 1978) n.p.

CHAPTER 3 - Loving God

1. John Piper, *Future Grace* (Sisters, OR: Multnomah Books, 1995), p. 9.

2. Adapted from Brother Lawrence *The Practice of the Presence of God* (Westwood, NJ: Fleming Revell, 1958), pp. 16-21.

3. Adapted from a radio broadcast by David Mains called "The Chapel of the Air." Part of a series titled "Going On a God Hunt."

CHAPTER 4 - Knowing God

1. J.I. Packer, *Knowing God*, p. 21.

2. Adapted from a message delivered by Waylon Moore, former pastor and currently a leader of discipleship training conferences.

3. Taken from a chapel message delivered by Robertson McQuilkin to the student body of Columbia International University, during Mr. McQuilkin's tenure as school president.

CHAPTER 5 - Helping Others to Know God
1. Leighton Ford, *The Christian Persuader* (New York, NY: Harper and Row, 1966), p. 39.

CHAPTER 6 - Seeking God through His Word
1. J. I. Packer, *Knowing God*, p. 16.
2. As quoted in *Welcome to the Church* (Littleton, CO: Lay Action Ministry Program, 1987), p. 59.
3. Ibid., p. 22

CHAPTER 7 - Seeking God through Prayer
1. Richard Foster, *Prayer: Finding the Heart's True Home* (San Francisco: Harper, 1992), p. 8.
2. Ibid., p. 179.

CHAPTER 8 - Seeking God through Time Alone with Him
1. Robert Munger, *My Heart, Christ's Home* (Downers Grove, IL: InterVarsity, 1986), pp. 15-16.
2. Powell, *Welcome to the Church*, p. 44.
3. Taken from a chapel message delivered by Robertson McQuilkin to the student body of Columbia International University, during Mr. McQuilkin's tenure as school president.

CHAPTER 9 - Seeking God through Other Christians
1. Bruce Milne, *We Belong Together: The Meaning of Fellowship* (Downers Grove, IL: InterVarsity Press, 1978), p. 19.
2. Charles Swindoll, *Living Beyond the Daily Grind*, Book II (Waco, TX: Word Books, 1988), p. 438.

CHAPTER 10 - Seeking God with a Clean Heart

1. Joe Aldrich, "Keeping Your Heart Beautiful," in *Secrets to Inner Beauty* (Santa Ana, CA: Vision House Publishers, 1977), pp. 39-45.
2. Ibid.
3. Ibid.
4. Ibid.

CHAPTER 11 - Seeking God with a Whole Heart
1. Wilbur Rees, as quoted by Tim Hansel, *When I Relax I Feel Guilty* (Elgin, IL: David C. Cook Publishers, 1979), p. 49.
2. Charles Swindoll, *Living above the Level of Mediocrity* (Waco, TX: Word Publishers, 1987), pp. 57-58.
3. Ibid, p. 11.

CHAPTER 12 - Looking Back . . . Going Forward
1. Bruce Larsen, *There's a Lot More to Health than Not Being Sick* (Waco, TX: Word Books, 1984), p. 74.
2. Bruce Wilkinson, *The Seven Laws of the Learner*, Textbook Edition (Sisters, OR: Multnomah Books, 1992), p. 198.
3. Swindoll, *Living above the Level of Mediocrity*, pp. 126, 133.